Avoiding Data Pitfalls

Avoiding Data Pitfalls

How to Steer Clear of Common Blunders When Working with Data and Presenting Analysis and Visualizations

Ben Jones

WILEY

Published by John Wiley & Sons, Inc., Hoboken, New Jersey.
Published simultaneously in Canada.

For general information on our other products and services or for technical support, please contact our Customer Care Department within the United States at (800) 762-2974, outside the United States at (317) 572-3993, or fax (317) 572-4002.

Wiley publishes in a variety of print and electronic formats and by print-on-demand. Some material included with standard print versions of this book may not be included in e-books or in print-on-demand. If this book refers to media such as a CD or DVD that is not included in the version you purchased, you may download this material at http://booksupport.wiley.com. For more information about Wiley products, visit www.wiley.com.

Library of Congress Cataloging-in-Publication Data

Names: Jones, Ben, 1978– author.
Title: Avoiding data pitfalls : how to steer clear of common blunders when
   working with data and presenting analysis and visualizations / Ben
   Jones.
Description: Hoboken, New Jersey : John Wiley & Sons, Inc., [2020] |
   Includes index.
Identifiers: LCCN 2019033232 (print) | LCCN 2019033233 (ebook) | ISBN
   9781119278160 (paperback) | ISBN 9781119278191 (adobe pdf) | ISBN
   9781119278177 (epub)
Subjects: LCSH: Information visualization. | Quantitative research.
Classification: LCC QA76.9.I52 J6639 2020 (print) | LCC QA76.9.I52
   (ebook) | DDC 001.4/226—dc23
LC record available at https://lccn.loc.gov/2019033232
LC ebook record available at https://lccn.loc.gov/2019033233

Cover Design: Wiley
Cover Image: © deomis/iStock.com

Printed in the United States of America.

V10014617_101019

Contents

Preface

There's a passage in *The Dhammapada*, which is a collection of sayings of the Buddha in verse form, which has this to say:

> *If you see someone wise, who can steer you away from the wrong path, follow that person, as you would one who can reveal hidden treasures. Only good can come out of it. Let them admonish, or instruct, or restrain you from what is wrong.*
> — The Dhammapada, *Verse 76*

Most ancient wisdom texts have a similar exhortation to find a wise person and follow their advice. If you listen to their words carefully, you'll avoid horrible mistakes and the associated pain and discomfort that these mistakes will cause in your life. We all need a mentor, guide, or guru from time to time.

Unfortunately, I may not be that wise person you're looking for. I'd say I'm more like a person who has taken his bumps and bruises while searching for such a wise individual myself. So I'm more like the person in the words to a favorite song of mine:

> *No, I don't claim to be a wise man, a poet or a saint. I'm just another man who's searching for a better way.*
> — Jon Bon Jovi, *"Bang a Drum"*

I figured it just might be helpful, however, to capture and convey the types of mistakes I've made, and seen others make, many times over the course of my data working career. I've worked with data in manufacturing and transactional environments, on the shop floor, in the boardroom, and in newsrooms all over the country, and I've trained and taught people how to work with data in corporate conference rooms, virtual chat rooms, and in the halls of academia, from coast to coast.

But who, exactly, am I trying to help with this book? Well, me, for one. Every time I write a blog post, record a tutorial, or craft a presentation, I find myself going back to these materials over and over. Whenever I do, I stop and wonder how the past version of myself was so much smarter than the current version of me, and I tip my hat for the favor.

And I hope it will be helpful for you. If you're starting out in your data journey, you'll come across many of these pitfalls, I promise you. My hope is that you'll be more likely to recognize them for what they are when you see them – sometimes from the top and other times from the bottom.

And if you've been working with data for some time, you'll read a section here or there, and you'll nod knowingly, glancing down at a scar or two that you earned by falling headfirst into the pit with me. And your brow may furrow when you read about other pitfalls, a sinking feeling coming over you that you may have made that mistake without recognizing it. If so, know that I feel your pain.

It's really important, though, that we learn to pick ourselves up and dust off our jeans, clean off those scuff marks, ice any bruises we may have suffered, and carry on, a bit wiser for the experience.

Equal in importance is that we show others the same grace. It's just too easy to get it wrong, and it's bound to happen. Even experts fall into data pitfalls on a fairly regular basis. Just like a well-worn path that marks the best route across a terrain, the more we admit and talk about our shortcomings, the less likely others are to fall into the same trap we fell into. We'll be leaving warning signs for them.

You and I may have to swallow our pride when we raise our hand and share the mea culpa, but we can think of it as a gift for future generations. They may shake their heads and wonder how we messed up so badly, but you and I will know that the only reason they've evolved as far as they have is that we paved the way for them with our blunders.

What's more important than the protection of my ego or yours is the evolution of our species into an efficient and effective data working force for the planet. We're not there, yet. Not even close.

I'd like to dedicate this book to my father, Richard Jones. My father had a truly wonderful mind, and, like the rest of us, he fell into many pitfalls in his life. When I confronted him about some things he had done that were particularly hurtful to me, he admitted it, and he apologized. I'll never forget that gift he gave me. It was very liberating.

I've been much better at admitting my own failures ever since – personal and professional. Thank you, Dad. I love you.

I signed the contract to write this book right before his health took a turn for the worse. He passed away of glioblastoma half a year later, and I lost all sight of the reason for wanting to write this book in the first place. My editors and the team at John Wiley & Sons were very gracious to me during this process. It took a while – four years to be exact – but eventually I rediscovered my passion for this topic and finished the book.

On the positive side, all that extra time meant that I was able to discover even more pitfalls to add to these chapters, mostly by falling into them.

So I hope this book proves to be helpful for you. May you stride forward onto the road paved with data, alert to pitfalls around every turn. May you show yourself compassion whenever you get it wrong, and may you share the lessons of mistakes made with others around you. Ultimately, may you reach great heights on the pathway, uncovering new treasures, solving pressing problems, and unlocking growth you never thought you'd find.

And if you bump into a truly wise data guru, will you give me their number? I'd appreciate it – I have a lot more to learn from them.

Chapter One

The Seven Types of Data Pitfalls

"You need to give yourself permission to be human."
—*Joyce Brothers*

Data pitfalls. Anyone who has worked with data has fallen into them many, many times. I certainly have. It's as if we've used data to pave the way for a better future, but the road we've made is filled with craters we just don't seem to notice until we're at the bottom looking up. Sometimes we fall into them and don't even know it. Finding out about it much later can be quite humbling.

If you've worked with data before, you know the feeling. You're giving an important presentation, your data is insightful beyond belief, your charts and graphs are impeccable and Tufte-compliant, the build to your grand conclusion is unassailable and awe-inspiring. And then that one guy in the back of the room – the guy with folded arms and furrowed brow – waits until the very end to ask you if you're aware that the database you're working with is fundamentally flawed, pulling the rug right out from underneath you, and plunging you to the bottom of yet another data pitfall. It's enough to make a poor data geek sweat bullets.

The nature of data pitfalls is that we have a particular blindness to them. It makes sense if you think about it. The human race hasn't needed to work with billions of records of data in the form of zeros and ones until the second half of the last century. Just a couple of decades later, though, our era is characterized by an ever-increasing abundance of data and a growing array of incredibly powerful tools. In many ways, our brains just haven't quite caught up yet.

These data pitfalls don't doom our every endeavor, though. Far from it. We've accomplished great things in this new era of data. We've mapped the human genome and begun to understand the complexity of the human brain, how its neurons interact so as to stimulate cognition. We've charted vast galaxies *out there* and we've come to a better understanding of geological and meteorological patterns *right here* on our own planet. Even in the simpler endeavors of life like holiday shopping, recommendation engines on e-commerce sites have evolved to be incredibly helpful. Our successes with data are too numerous to list.

But our slipups with data are mounting as well. Misuse of data has led to great harm and loss. From the colossal failure of Wall Street quants and their models in the financial crisis of the previous decade to the parable of Google Flu Trends and its lesson in data-induced hubris,[1] our use of data isn't always so successful. In fact, sometimes it's downright disastrous.

Why is that? Simply because we have a tendency to make certain kinds of mistakes time and time again. Noticing those mistakes early in the process is quite easy – just as long as it's someone else who's making them. When I'm the one committing the blunder, it seems I don't find out until that guy in the back of the room launches his zinger.

---

[1] http://gking.harvard.edu/files/gking/files/0314policyforumff.pdf.

And like our good friend and colleague, we're all quite adept at spotting the screw-ups of other people, aren't we? I had an early lesson in this haphazard trade. In my seventh-grade science fair exhibition, a small group of budding student scientists had a chance to walk around with the judges and explain our respective science fair projects while the other would-be blue-ribbon winners listened along. The judges, wanting to encourage dialogue and inquisitiveness, encouraged the students to also ask questions after each presentation. In spite of the noble intention behind this prompting, we basically just used the opportunity to poke holes in the methods and analysis of our competition. Kids can be cruel.

I don't do science fair projects anymore, unlike many other parents at my sons' schools, but I do work with data a lot. And I work with others who work with data a lot, too. In all of my data wrangling, data remixing, data analyzing, data visualizing, and data surmising, I've noticed that there are specific types of pitfalls that exist on the road to data paradise.

In fact, in my experience, I've found that the pitfalls we fall into can be grouped into one of seven categories.

Seven Types of Data Pitfalls

Pitfall 1: Epistemic Errors: How We Think About Data

What can data tell us? Maybe even more importantly, what *can't* it tell us? Epistemology is the field of philosophy that deals with the theory of knowledge – what's a reasonable belief versus what is just opinion. We often approach data with the wrong mind-set and assumptions, leading to errors all along the way, regardless of what chart type we choose, such as:

- Assuming that the data we are using is a perfect reflection of reality
- Forming conclusions about the future based on historical data only
- Seeking to use data to verify a previously held belief rather than to test it to see whether it's actually false

Avoiding epistemic errors and making sure we are thinking clearly about what's reasonable and what's unreasonable is an important foundation for successful data analysis.

Pitfall 2: Technical Traps: How We Process Data

Once we've decided to use data to help solve a particular problem, we have to gather it, store it, join it with other data sets, transform it, clean it up, and get it in the right shape. Doing so can result in:

- Dirty data with mismatching category levels and data entry typos
- Units of measurement or date fields that aren't consistent or compatible
- Bringing together disparate data sets and getting nulls or duplicated rows that skew analysis

These steps can be complex and messy, but accurate analysis depends on doing them right. Sometimes the truth contained within data gets "lost in translation," and it's possible to plow ahead and make decisions without even knowing we're dealing with a seriously flawed data set.

Pitfall 3: Mathematical Miscues: How We Calculate Data

Working with data almost always involves calculations – doing math with the quantitative data we have at our disposal:

- Summing at various levels of aggregation
- Calculating rates or ratios
- Working with proportions and percentages
- Dealing with different units

These are just a few examples of how we take data fields that exist and create new data fields out of them. Just like in grade school, it's very possible to get the math wrong. These mistakes can be quite costly – an error of this type led to the loss of a $125 million Mars orbiter in 1999.[2] That was more like falling into a black hole than a pitfall.

Pitfall 4: Statistical Slipups: How We Compare Data

"There are lies, damned lies, and statistics." This saying usually implies that someone is fudging the numbers to mislead others, but we can just as often be lying to ourselves when it comes to statistics. Whether we're talking about descriptive or inferential statistics, the pitfalls abound:

- Are the measures of central tendency or variation that we're using leading us astray?
- Are the samples we're working with representative of the population we wish to study?
- Are the means of comparison we're using valid and statistically sound?

These pitfalls are numerous and particularly hard to spot on the horizon, because they deal with a way of thinking that even experts can get wrong sometimes. "Simple random samples" can be anything but simple to get right, and just ask a data guru to explain what a "p-value" means in layman's terms sometime.

Pitfall 5: Analytical Aberrations: How We Analyze Data

Analysis is at the heart of every data working endeavor. It's the means by which we draw conclusions and make decisions. There are many people who have "analyst" in their job title, but in truth, data analysis is a task that virtually everyone performs at one point or another. Data analysis has reached new heights, but we can also sink to new lows, like:

---

[2] http://www.cnn.com/TECH/space/9909/30/mars.metric.02/.

- Over-fitting our models to the historical data
- Missing important signals in the data
- Extrapolating or interpolating in ways that don't make sense
- Using metrics that don't really matter at all

Was it really reasonable to assume search trends could let us accurately predict the number of people who will get the flu, even while search algorithms are constantly changing and the searching population reacts to inputs like media hype and search engine recommendations?

Pitfall 6: Graphical Gaffes: How We Visualize Data

These are the mistakes that are most commonly noticed and talked about. Why? Because they're the visual ones. They're there for all to see and gaze upon in horror. You know the ones I'm talking about: dizzying pie charts with dozens of slices, misleading bar charts with y-axes that start at half of the maximum value. Luckily, these pitfalls are well documented, and can be identified by asking a handful of questions:

- Did we choose a sufficiently suitable chart type for the task at hand?
- If a point is being made, is it shown clearly, or do we have to strain to see it?
- Are we making use of rules of thumb without being unduly limited by them?

Sure, getting the chart type perfectly right is useless if we've fallen into one of the first five pitfalls above, but what a shame it is when we successfully execute on the whole routine up until this point only to botch the landing.

Pitfall 7: Design Dangers: How We Dress up Data

As humans, we really appreciate good design. We drive to work in well-designed automobiles, with all of the controls in the right place, and sit at our desk in ergonomic chairs that conform gracefully to the contours of our bodies. Why would we want to sit there and open our browser to look at some garish infographic or clunky data dashboard? Design matters.

- Do our color choices confuse our audience or do they make things clearer to them?
- Have we used our creativity to judiciously embellish charts, or have we missed out on a great opportunity to include aesthetic components that add value?
- Are the visual objects we have created easy to interact with, or do they befuddle the user?

Getting these design elements right can actually mean the difference between our audience paying close attention to our message and totally ignoring us and paying attention to something else instead.

These seven pitfalls are like seven deadly sins – any one of them can make or break our data-working endeavor. But there's no sense in fearing them. We'd like to learn how to recover quickly when we find ourselves at the bottom of one, or, even better, learn to avoid them altogether. How do we do that?

Avoiding the Seven Pitfalls

When we come across a pitfall on a particular path in the real world, we'd like to think that there is a nice, helpful sign pointing it out to us and warning us of the danger, like the one on the Coal Creek Falls trail near my home in Bellevue, Washington (Figure 1.1).

But with data pitfalls, such helpful warning signs don't typically exist, do they? It's up to us to know these cognitive, procedural, and communicative pitfalls well and to know why it's so easy to fall into one. Awareness and mindfulness are the keys. If we aren't familiar with these nasty traps – what they look like, how to spot them, their telltale signs – then we're much more likely to fall into them. That much is obvious.

FIGURE 1.1   An ominous warning sign of a pitfall on the path to Coal Creek Falls in Bellevue, Washington.

But merely knowing about them often isn't enough. Even the sagest of data experts falls into these well-hidden traps from time to time. We need some helpful tips and trusty guides to help us along the way.

Starting in the following chapter, "Epistemic Errors," we'll begin collecting practical tips that will help us avoid each of the seven pitfalls so that we can remain on the straight and narrow data highway. By the end of our discussion of the seventh pitfall in Chapter 8, "Design Dangers," we'll have a full checklist that we can use to serve as a kind of trail map for our journey.

"I've Fallen and I Can't Get Up"

The fact is, though, we don't often have time to run through a comprehensive checklist before forging ahead on our data journey. The pressing demands of business and the fast-paced environments in which we operate routinely present us with shortened deadlines and the need to produce insights from data in less time than we really need.

In these cases, we may have no choice but to press ahead, but at least we can use the "Avoiding Data Pitfalls Checklist" that we will present in the final chapter as a postmortem tool to identify our particular propensities, and to find out which pitfalls we find ourselves falling into time and again.

And it's going to happen. I promise that you will fall into one or more of these pitfalls in the very near future. So will your colleagues. So will I. I probably fell into more than one of them in this book itself. As a species, we're still learning how to change the way we think to suit this relatively new medium.

On an evolutionary scale, interacting with large spreadsheets and databases is not just new, it's brand new. Anatomically modern humans first appear in the fossil record around 195,000 years ago in Africa, and pioneering computer scientist Alan Turing set out the idea of the modern computer in his seminal 1936 paper, roughly 80 years ago.[3] That means we've been acclimating to the computing era for a grand total of 0.04% of human history. That's the fraction of a day that occurs in the last 35 seconds, between 11:59:25 p.m. and 12:00:00 a.m.

Okay, then it's going to happen. So how do we react when it does? We should see these mistakes as an unavoidable step in the process of developing a keen sense of navigation.

Do you remember learning about bloodletting, the ill-conceived practice of withdrawing blood from a patient to treat illness and disease? In classrooms around the world, the youth of our era scoff at the folly of this barbaric practice as they are taught about it year after year. But it was a common medical technique for 2,000 years, from antiquity until the late nineteenth century.

---

[3] https://www.cs.virginia.edu/~robins/Turing_Paper_1936.pdf

Just like our forebears, our generation makes many boneheaded mistakes on a routine basis that future generations will find baffling. It's my hope that falling into data pitfalls will be among those human propensities that our progeny find inexplicable in future generations.

So what happens when we find ourselves in the bottom of a nasty data pitfall? What do we do then? Our inclination is to pretend it never happened, cover up the mistake, and hope no one finds out. This is the opposite of what we should do:

- First, try to get out: fix your mistake.
- Second, put a notch on your checklist next to the pitfall into which you fell.
- Third, tell everyone about what happened.

This process, as self-flagellating as it sounds, will help us all grow the muscle of effective data working. To ensure others can follow this process as well, we'll need to refrain from vilifying those who fall into data pitfalls. Remember, it not only could have been you, it *will* be you sometime down the road.

Chapter Two

Pitfall 1: Epistemic Errors

"Everybody gets so much information all day long that they lose their common sense."

—*Gertrude Stein*

How We Think About Data

Epistemology is the branch of philosophy that deals with the nature, origin, and scope of our knowledge. It comes from the Greek words *episteme* (knowledge) and *logos* (word/speech) – knowledge speech, or, in other words, talking about knowledge.

Let's talk about knowledge as it relates to working with data. But first, why spend any time on this at all? A fair question, since clearly practitioners of many disciplines ignore the fundamental principles underlying their area of focus. Take driving an automobile, for example. Most drivers can't explain how the internal combustion engine works, or how the batteries in their electric vehicle function. But that doesn't stop them from driving around town, does it?

But working with data isn't like driving a car in this respect. It's more like cooking. In order to do it well, we need a working knowledge of the ways heat is transferred to food over time and how different flavors combine to produce a final result. We can't just start throwing ingredients together at random and hope to make a great dish. That's just one of the things I learned living with roommates in college, by the way.

But that's what happens when we start cooking things up with data before we have an understanding of the basic principles of knowledge. Epistemology is our data cookbook of sorts. Let's see what's in it.

Pitfall 1A: The Data-Reality Gap

The first epistemic principle to embrace is that there is always a gap between our data and the real world. We fall headfirst into a pitfall when we forget that this gap exists, that our data isn't a perfect reflection of the real-world phenomena it's representing. Do people really fail to remember this? It sounds so basic. How could anyone fall into such an obvious trap?

I'm not exaggerating when I say that I fail to avoid this trap almost every single time. The first pitfall is a gaping hole and pretty much every one falls right into it at first.

It works like this: I get my hands on some data and I perform some analysis, but I don't stop to think about where the data came from, who collected it, what it tells me, and, importantly, what it doesn't tell me.

It's easy when working with data to treat it as reality itself rather than data collected about reality. Here are some examples:

- It's not crime, it's *reported* crime.
- It's not the outer diameter of a mechanical part, it's the *measured* outer diameter.

- It's not how the public feels about a topic, it's how *people who responded* to the survey *are willing to say* they feel.

You get the picture. This distinction may seem like a technicality, and sometimes it might be (the number of home runs Hank Aaron "reportedly" hit?), but it can also be a very big deal. Let's see some examples of how we can fall into this pitfall.

Example 1: All the Meteorites We Don't See

The Meteoritical Society provides data for 34,513 meteorites that struck the surface of the earth between 2,500 BCE and 2012.[1] If you and I were to take this figure and run with it, we might make a number of incorrect assumptions that stem from the first data pitfall we're considering together.

Let's look more closely to get a better understanding of the impact of falling into this pitfall.

A friend of mine, Ramon Martinez, created a map (Figure 2.1) depicting where each of these 34,513 meteorites had struck the surface of the earth.

What do you notice about the data now that we're looking at it on a map? Doesn't it seem uncanny that meteorites are so much more likely to hit the surface of the earth where there's land, as opposed to where there's ocean? And what about areas like the Amazon (not the one in Seattle), or Greenland, or parts of Central Africa? Is there some kind of shield over those areas, or some deity protecting those areas from damage? We humans are great at coming up with bullshit theories like this, aren't we?

The explanation is obvious, and Ramon actually gives it to us right in the title at the top of the visualization: "Every Recorded Meteorite Impact." In order for a meteorite to be in the database, it had to be recorded. And in order for it to be recorded, it had to be observed

[1] https://www.lpi.usra.edu/meteor/metbull.php.

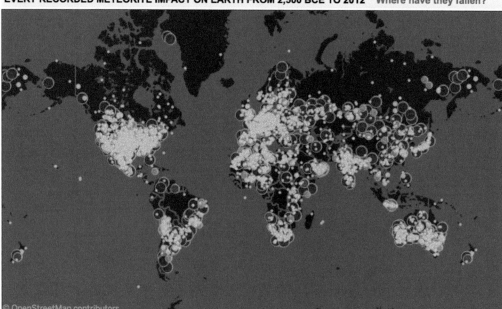

FIGURE 2.1   Meteorite strikes by Ramon Martinez.

Source: Ramon Martinez, https://public.tableau.com/profile/ramon.martinez#!/vizhome/meteorite_fall_on_
earth/Meteoritefallonearthvisualized.

by someone. Not just anyone, but someone who knew whom to tell about it. And the person they told had to be faithful in carrying out their job of recording it. That's much more likely to occur in areas of higher population density of developed nations.

The map, then, isn't showing us where meteorites are more likely to strike the earth. It's telling us where meteorites are more likely to have fallen (in the past), and were observed by someone who reported it to someone who recorded it faithfully.

Now, that's a mouthful, isn't it? And you may roll your eyes and say it's all just a bunch of technicalities. But think again about the 34,513 figure. If we began with this figure, and if we assumed like I did at first that experts or enthusiasts observe and record every single meteorite strike no matter where it falls, then we'd have a pretty inaccurate idea of how often this kind of event actually occurs on the planet.

It's not that the data that the Meteoritical Society provides is wrong; it's just that there's a gap between the number of meteorites that have actually hit the earth since 2,500 BCE, and those that have been observed, reported, and recorded. It's safe to say that there's a massive difference between the unknowable total count and the number in the database. After all, about 71% of the earth's surface is covered by water, and some of the land itself is also completely uninhabited.

But the number of meteorites that are missing from the database because they aren't seen due to geographic reasons pales in comparison to the ones that are missing due to lack of historical record-keeping. If we look at a dot plot (Figure 2.2) that shows the number of meteorites recorded by calendar year – each year having its own dot – we see that records weren't kept until the twentieth century.

There's a huge gap in time between the oldest known meteorite (traced to Iraq, from about 2,500 BCE) and the second oldest (traced to Poland, from about 600 BCE). No year prior to 1800 includes more than two recorded meteorites. And then in the twentieth century the numbers increase dramatically, with over 3,000 recorded in 1979

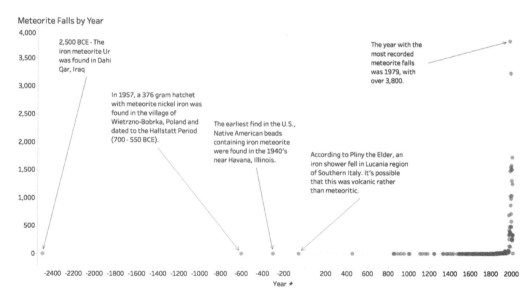

FIGURE 2.2   A timeline of recorded meteorite falls, 2,500 BCE–2012

and 1988 alone. It's safe to assume that ancient times saw a plethora of meteorites as well; it's just that humans didn't see them. Or if they did, they had nowhere to record it – at least not in a place that was preserved over the ages.

Example 2: Are Earthquakes Really on the Rise?

Let's consider another geological phenomenon: earthquakes. I grew up in Southern California, and I remember the early morning of January 17, 1994, quite vividly. At 4:31 a.m., a magnitude 6.7 earthquake struck the San Fernando Valley region of Los Angeles, killing 57 people, injuring more than 8,700, and causing widespread damage.

The United States Geological Survey provides an Earthquake Archive Search form that lets visitors obtain a list of historical earthquakes that meet various criteria.[2] A query of earthquakes of magnitude 6.0 and above from 1900 to 2013 yields a somewhat alarming line plot (Figure 2.3).

Are we really to believe that earthquakes have increased in frequency by this much? Obviously not. The world that measured and collected earthquakes in the early twentieth century was very different than the one that did so in the last decade. Comparisons across decades, and even within some decades (the 1960s, for example), aren't "apples-to-apples" due to the changes in technology.

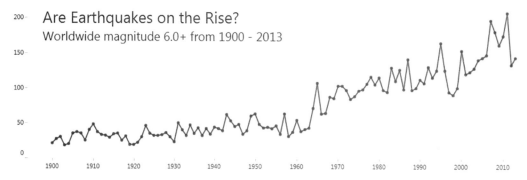

Are Earthquakes on the Rise?
Worldwide magnitude 6.0+ from 1900 - 2013

FIGURE 2.3   A line plot of earthquakes of magnitude of 6.0 and greater.

_____

[2] https://earthquake.usgs.gov/earthquakes/search/.

If we separate the line plot by magnitude and add annotations that describe advances in seismology, we see that the rise is only in the smaller group (magnitude 6.0–6.9), and coincides with dramatic improvements in instrumentation (Figure 2.4).

It's safe to say that the rise in recorded earthquakes is primarily due to the improvements in our ability to detect them. There may also be an upward trend in actual earthquakes over this time, but it's impossible for us to know for sure due to the continual changes in the quality of the measurement system. For all we know, the actual trend could be a decreasing one.

When it comes to earthquakes, the gap between data and reality is getting smaller. As much as this is a marvelous technical development to be applauded, a by-product of our advancement is that it's difficult to discern historical trends.

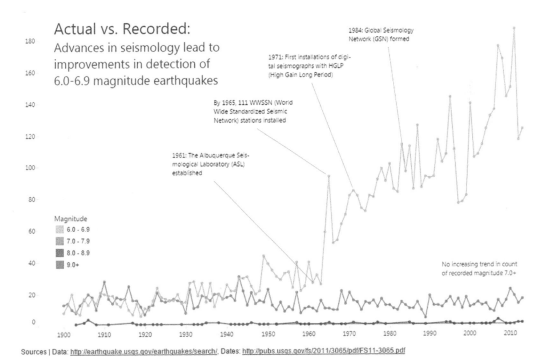

Sources | Data: http://earthquake.usgs.gov/earthquakes/search/. Dates: http://pubs.usgs.gov/fs/2011/3065/pdf/FS11-3065.pdf

FIGURE 2.4   Breaking out worldwide earthquakes by magnitude group.

The fundamental epistemic problem is that the "data-reality gap" is dramatically changing over the time period we're considering. It's hard to know for sure exactly how many magnitude 6.0 earthquakes we missed in any particular year.

Let's look at another example: counting bicycles that cross a bridge.

Example 3: Counting Bicycles

Every day on my way to work from 2013 to 2015 I would walk across the Fremont Bridge in Seattle, Washington. It's a bright blue and orange double-leaf bascule bridge that was built in 1917. Since it sits so close to the water, it opens on average 35 times a day, which supposedly makes it the most opened drawbridge in the United States. Here's what it looks like (Figure 2.5).

Seattle is a city of avid bicyclists, and the City of Seattle Department of Transportation has installed two inductive loops on the pedestrian/bicycle pathways of the bridge that are designed to count the number of bicycles that cross the bridge in either direction, all

FIGURE 2.5 The Fremont Bridge as seen from the Aurora Bridge in Seattle, Washington.

day every day. The city also provides hourly counts going back to October 2, 2012, at data.seattle.gov.[3] Downloading this data and visualizing it yields the timeline in Figure 2.6.

I showed this timeline during a presentation at a luncheon of marketing researchers not far from the bridge one day, and I asked the attendees what they thought of these spikes in late April 2014. In that moment, I had no idea what had caused them.

A few ideas quickly sprang from the crowd. Was it "bike to work day"? Maybe the weather was abnormally beautiful and everyone got bike fever at the same time. It seemed strange that there was only a spike on one side of the bridge but not the other, though. How did they get home? Was there an actual spike that gave them all flat tires so they couldn't ride home? Or, maybe there was an organized bicycle race or club event that involved a looping route where the

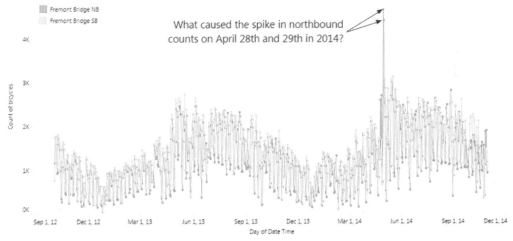

FIGURE 2.6 A time series of the counts of bicycles crossing the Fremont bridge, October 2012–December 2014.

---

[3] https://data.seattle.gov/Transportation/Fremont-Bridge-Hourly-Bicycle-Counts-by-Month-Octo/65db-xm6k.

riders crossed the water in another place instead of the riders turning around and coming back over the Fremont Bridge on the way back.

Notice how each of these ideas are based on the assumption that there actually *were* more bikes that crossed the bridge on those two days. No one in the room thought to question that basic assumption, myself included. We collectively shrugged our shoulders and I moved on with my presentation.

About 20 minutes later, one of the attendees in the back of the audience held up his smart phone (presenting is such a treacherous endeavor, these days) and shouted out that he found the reason for the spikes. It was a case of equipment error.

The counter had glitched for a period of time in April of that year, but only the counter on the eastbound side of the bridge (labeled "Fremont Bridge NB" in the data set for some reason). You can read all the details of these anomalous readings and the correspondence between a local blogger and a city employee at the Seattle Bike Blog.[4] The title of the blog post says it all: "Monday appears to smash Fremont Bridge bike counter record – UPDATE: Probably not."

According to correspondence between the blogger and the city employee published in updates to the blog post, there were actually four hour-long spikes in bicycle counts on the mornings of April 23, 25, 28, and 29. If you look closely at the timeline in Figure 2.6, you'll see the higher values in the blue line just before the huge spike as well. They never figured out what was wrong with the counter, if anything, but they validated that it was working properly and replaced some hardware and the battery.

What's interesting is that if you go to download this data today, you won't see the four daily spikes at all. They have adjusted the data, and the abnormally high values have been replaced with "typical volumes." Fascinating.

---

[4] https://www.seattlebikeblog.com/2014/04/29/monday-appears-to-smash-fremont-bridge-bike-counter-record/.

What really stuck with me was the fact that everyone in the room – myself included – immediately started proposing root causes from inside a specific box, and none of us thought to think outside of that box. The box in which we were stuck has a simple equation that describes it: data = reality. I find myself in that box over and over again. Every time I do, it makes me laugh at how easy it is to fall into this pitfall when working with data.

Let's consider yet another example of this first epistemic pitfall: counting Ebola deaths.

Example 4: When Cumulative Counts Go Down

In 2014, the whole world watched in horror as Ebola ravaged West Africa. During the crisis, the World Health Organization (WHO) provided data about fatalities in weekly situation reports.

Let's take a look at a timeline of cumulative deaths from Ebola as reported by the WHO and the Centers for Disease Control (CDC) from March 2014 through the end of that year (Figure 2.7). Notice the drops in cumulative death counts – the handful of times when the lines slope *downward*.

At first blush, this seems somewhat odd. How can there be fewer total people dead from the disease on one day than there were at the end of the previous day? The way I've worded the question shows that I've already fallen into the pitfall.

Let's ask it a different way: How can the total number of reported deaths due to the disease decrease from one day to the next?

Of course, it makes perfect sense: the task of diagnosing disease and ascertaining causes of death in some of the more remote locations, where the equipment and staff are often severely limited, must be incredibly difficult.

And the cause of death of any particular person isn't always so obvious to the professionals producing the figures. Often test

Ebola deaths in West Africa, 2014

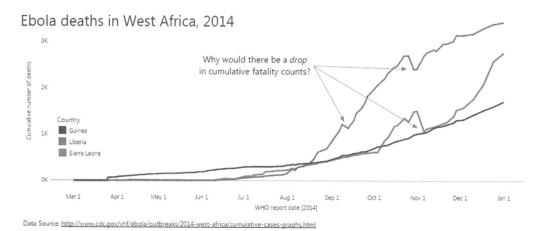

Data Source: http://www.cdc.gov/vhf/ebola/outbreaks/2014-west-africa/cumulative-cases-graphs.html

FIGURE 2.7   Cumulative timeline of Ebola fatality count in West Africa, 2014.

results that are received days or even weeks later can change the recorded cause of death. In the case of a fast-moving pandemic, guesses have to be made that are proven either true or false at a later point in time.

That's exactly why, if you read the WHO situation report, you'll notice that they classify cases as "suspected," "probable," and "confirmed." The criteria are shown in Figure 2.8.

The WHO and CDC actually do a very good job of speaking clearly about "reported" cases (the December 31 WHO situation report includes the word "reported" no less than 61 times).

I don't bring up this example to criticize the people or organizations involved with fighting and documenting the Ebola outbreak. Far from it. If anything, I commend their heroic efforts at fighting the disease and caring for those who were suffering and dying. And I commend them for clearly communicating to us the uncertainty inherent in their reporting of the data. But you can see how easy it would be for someone who downloaded the data, like me, to be confused by what I saw.

ANNEX 1: CATEGORIES USED TO CLASSIFY EBOLA CASES
Ebola cases are classified as suspected, probable, or confirmed depending on whether they meet certain criteria (table 3).

Table 3: Ebola case-classification criteria

Classification	Criteria
Suspected	Any person, alive or dead, who has (or had) sudden onset of high fever and had contact with a suspected, probable or confirmed Ebola case, or a dead or sick animal OR any person with sudden onset of high fever and at least three of the following symptoms: headache, vomiting, anorexia/ loss of appetite, diarrhoea, lethargy, stomach pain, aching muscles or joints, difficulty swallowing, breathing difficulties, or hiccup; or any person with unexplained bleeding OR any sudden, unexplained death.
Probable	Any suspected case evaluated by a clinician OR any person who died from 'suspected' Ebola and had an epidemiological link to a confirmed case but was not tested and did not have laboratory confirmation of the disease.
Confirmed	A probable or suspected case is classified as confirmed when a sample from that person tests positive for Ebola virus in the laboratory.

FIGURE 2.8   World Health Organization classification table of Ebola cases.

It turns out that classifying diseases and deaths in chaotic conditions can be tricky business indeed. This example merely demonstrates that the gap between data and reality can exist even when the stakes are high, and when the whole world is watching.

That's because this gap always exists. It's not a question of whether there's a gap, it's a question of how big it is.

Remember the supposedly trivial example of Hank Aaron's "reported" home run tally that I mentioned in passing earlier? Well, he hit an astounding 755 home runs over the course of his career in Major League Baseball, which stood as a record for 33 years. But what about the six home runs he hit in the playoffs, when it mattered the most? Or the two home runs he hit in the All-Star games in which he played while representing the National League in 1971 and 1972? And let's talk about the five home runs he hit in 26 official games while playing professionally for the Indianapolis Clowns of the Negro American Leagues prior to joining the Atlanta Braves. Shouldn't those count too? They're not incorporated into the official tally, which only includes regular season home runs hit in the MLB (Major League Baseball). But one could make the argument that those additional 13 home runs that he hit while playing professional baseball should bring his official career tally to 768.

There's always a gap.

Pitfall 1B: All Too Human Data

So let's recap. In Pitfall 1A, we saw data-reality gaps that result from measurement systems that change in resolution over time (seismology), have unknown glitches (bicycle counters), involve human-generated counts with missing data (meteorites), misclassified and later corrected data (Ebola deaths), and uncertain data due to unstated and unclear criteria (Hank Aaron's home runs).

But there's another type of gap that we humans create very frequently when we record values that we ourselves measure and then manually key in: we round, we fudge, and we guesstimate. We're not perfect, and we certainly don't record data with perfect precision.

The first example of rounding in human-keyed data that I'd like to look at is shown in Figure 2.9. It's the number of minutes past the hour that pilots provide when they report to the FAA that their aircraft struck wildlife at a particular moment on the runway or in flight. Now, I'm not familiar with the process that these pilots follow when they capture and report these incidents, but I'm willing to bet from looking at this chart that they're either writing down, dictating to someone, or keying in the time of day.

Of course, we know that the likelihood of an airplane hitting a bird or other creature doesn't change as a function of the number of minutes past the hour in this way. It's not as if the clock changes

Reported strikes by minute of the hour, non-null values

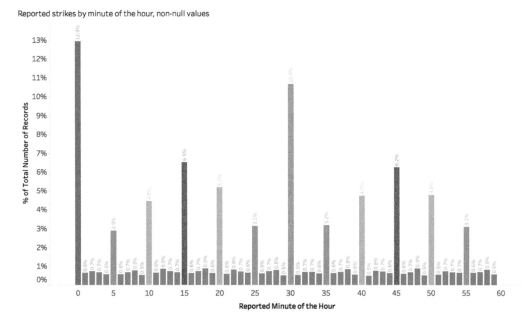

FIGURE 2.9   Example of rounding in human-keyed data.

from 1:04 p.m. to 1:05 p.m. and then suddenly the actual frequency of wildlife strikes more than quadruples. The dramatic rise in the columns is due to our tendency to round time when we glance at a watch or a clock. We see 1:04 and we write down 1:05, or, heck with it, we just call it 1:00 even – close enough, right? Pilots are just like us.

If this data had been generated by some sort of sensing mechanism mounted to the aircraft that automatically logged each strike, and included a time-date stamp with each record, you can bet this triangular pattern would completely disappear. And it's not like data created by such a nonhuman measurement system would be perfect, either. It would have its own unique quirks, idiosyncrasies, and patterns imposed by the equipment itself. But it wouldn't round like this – not unless we programmed it to. And in that case, there wouldn't be any nonrounded time entries at all.

What's fascinating to me, though, is the geometric regularity of this chart. Think about it: the plot comes from over 85,000 reported wildlife strikes that took place over the course of 18 years. Data provided by thousands and thousands of individual pilots all over the country over almost two decades ended up producing this pattern that feels like it was generated by a mathematical formula. Just take a look at how the column heights reach up to very interesting frequency lines (Figure 2.10).

And it's not just wildlife strikes that produce this pattern. Here's data that my friend Jay Lewis collected that shows the minutes past the hour recorded for the first 1,976 diaper changings of his child (Figure 2.11). Doesn't the pattern look familiar? Now that's what I call dirty data.

We do this kind of fudging or rounding when we report other quantitative variables too, not just with time. Let's look at another example of this kind of human-keyed rounding behavior (Figure 2.12).

The weights of NBA players from the 2017–18 season can be plotted using a histogram, and at first blush, if we use a bin size of 10 pounds, we don't see any evidence of rounding or lack of precision whatsoever.

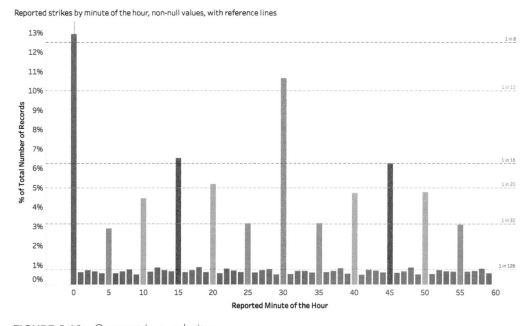

Reported strikes by minute of the hour, non-null values, with reference lines

FIGURE 2.10   Geometric regularity.

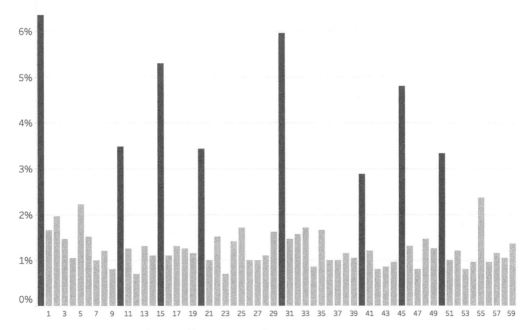

Diapers changed by minute of timestamp, 5/1/2018 to 10/29/2018

FIGURE 2.11 Diapers changed by minute of timestamp.

Let's look a little bit deeper, though. What happens if we change the bin size from 10 pounds to 1 pound? Now instead of grouping players in bins of 10 pounds (all six players with weights between 160 and 169 pounds get grouped together, the 20 players with weights between 170 and 179 pounds get grouped together, etc.), we create a bin for each integer weight: the two players with 160 pounds are grouped together, the single player with 161 pounds gets his own group, and so on.

When we do this, another interesting pattern emerges that tells us something's going on with the measurement system here. The process of capturing and recording data is resulting in a fingerprint of human-keyed data again, this time with a different pattern than the one we saw when we looked at time data (Figure 2.13).

What's going on here? Almost half of the players have a listed weight that's divisible by 10, and almost 3 out of every 4 players

2017-18 NBA Player Weights (bin size = 10lbs)

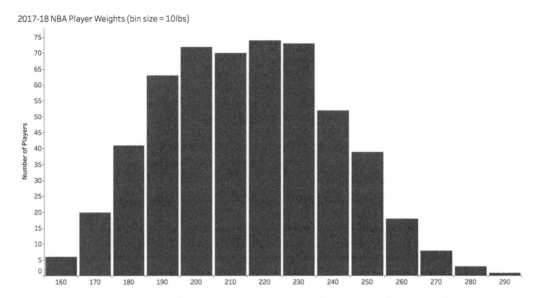

FIGURE 2.12   A histogram of NBA player weights, with bin size of 10 pounds.

(74%) have a weight that's divisible by 5. There are players, though, with listed weights that don't fall into these neat buckets. Just over 1 in 4 (26% to be precise) has a listed weight that isn't divisible by 5, such as the three players listed at 201 pounds, for example – clearly a number that begs to be rounded, if any does. But players with weights like this are in the minority.

Of course, the actual weights of the players, if we were to weigh them all and capture the readings automatically using a digital scale, wouldn't produce this type of "chunky" data, would it? There might be some grouping of players around certain values, but this is clearly caused by humans reporting approximate values.

I'm also quite certain that the doctors and trainers employed by the basketball teams have much more granular biometric data about these players than the figures posted to rosters published on the Internet. But the processes that produce the particular values that you and I can see on the web definitely show fingerprints of human-keyed data.

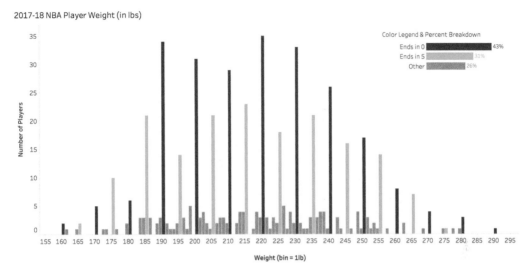

2017-18 NBA Player Weight (in lbs)

FIGURE 2.13 An adjusted histogram of NBA player weights, this time with bin size of 1 pound.

Let's look elsewhere. If we scrape the online rosters of over 2,800 North American professional football players who were listed as active on preseason rosters before the 2018 season, we see similar grouping around weights divisible by 5 and 10, but not quite to the same degree; only half of the players fall into these neat buckets, and the other half fall into buckets not divisible by 5 or 10 (Figure 2.14).

The measurement system and process of capturing and recording weights of American football players and publishing these figures to online rosters is twice as likely to result in a value that isn't divisible by 5. It could be that player weight is much more of a critical factor in this sport, and therefore one that's more closely tracked and monitored. But that's just a guess, if I'm honest. We'd have to map out the measurement system for both leagues to figure out the source of the difference in resolution.

And you may say, well – who cares? We're talking about a minute here or there in the pilot wildlife strike example, and a pound here or there in the basketball player weight example. But the thing is, sometimes that level of precision really does matter, and the data might reflect that.

2018 NFL Active Players (2,875 players)

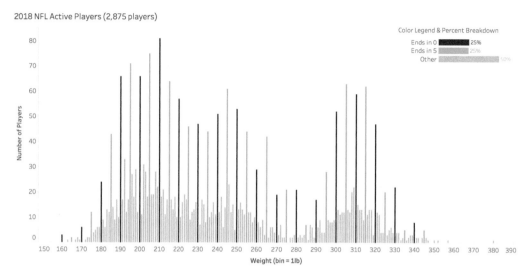

FIGURE 2.14   A histogram of weights of North American football players.

There's actually a perfect scenario that shows what the data looks like when the precision of player weight data matters a whole lot more than online team rosters. Every year, American football players who are entering the professional draft are tracked, scrutinized, and measured by team scouts with extreme precision in an event called the NFL Combine. These players are put through a gauntlet of physical performance tests, and practically everything except the number of hairs on their head are counted and measured. What type of weight profile does this event produce?

If we look at the 1,305 players who entered the Combine from 2013 through 2018 and who ended up playing in the NFL, we find that more than 3 in 4 players have recorded and published weights that don't end in either 0 or 5 (Figure 2.15).

The lack of a human-keyed, rounded process is evident. If we look at the frequency of player weight by last digit, we see that the Combine produces a very uniform distribution, and players have been no more likely to have a recorded weight ending in 0 or 5 as ending in any other number:

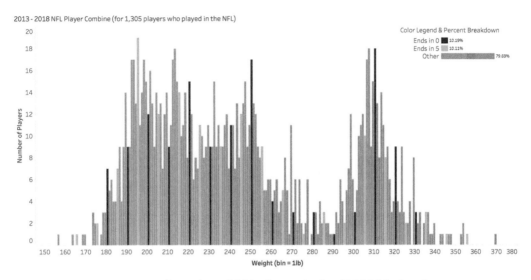

FIGURE 2.15   Histogram of weights of 283 players in the 2018 NFL Combine.

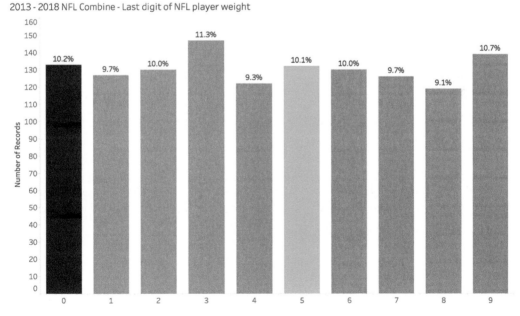

FIGURE 2.16   Histogram of the number (and %) of players having weights ending in 0 through 9.

So what does this mean? Well, measurement systems can be very different, even when they measure the exact same variable (weight) of the same type of object (American football players). Some measurement systems involve a high amount of rounding, fudging, and guesstimating by humans, some involve less, and some don't involve much at all. We can't know which we're dealing with unless we obtain a deep understanding of the measurement system process and a deep understanding of the data that it produces.

When we obtain such understanding, we'll be a little bit closer to knowing where the data-reality gap is coming from this time.

Pitfall 1C: Inconsistent Ratings

The Internet thrives on ratings generated by humans. Just in the past month, I've been prompted to provide a rating for a greasy spoon (but amazing) New Orleans breakfast restaurant, countless car share rides, a few meditations I listened to on a popular app, three audiobooks, a print book written by none other than my own mother – you name it. And that just scratches the surface.

Before we leave the section on human imperfections in the data collection process, let's talk bananas. Yes, bananas.

I like to run silly polls on social media now and then. Sometimes I throw my followers a little curveball with my polls, like the one in Figure 2.17:

So what this says is that 1 in 5 people who responded to a poll on social media say that they're unwilling to respond to a poll on social media. Another 1 in 3 respond that they prefer not to say whether or not they're willing to respond. Hmm …

But I digress. Bananas. I ran another not-so-scientific little poll this past year asking my social media pals to rate a series of 10 banana photos on a ripeness scale. Each photo was classified by respondents as either unripe, almost ripe, ripe, very ripe, or overripe. These five different categories of ripeness have not been vetted by the National Association of Banana Raters, or any other such body, if one exists. They came from my brain – clearly a surprising place.

Ben Jones ☑ @DataRemixed · Aug 6
Q: Are you willing to respond to polls you see on social media?

45% Yes, I'm willing to

21% No, I'm not willing to

34% I prefer not to say

253 votes • Final results

10:06 AM - 7 Aug 2018

FIGURE 2.17 Social media poll.

Figure 2.18 presents the photos of the bananas I showed them. Each photo was shown once, and every respondent was shown the exact same bananas in the exact same order.

What will shock no one is that people don't tend to think of banana ripeness quite the same way. A banana that's ripe to me may be considered almost ripe to you, and it's most definitely overripe to someone else.

What was mildly startling to me, though, was just how differently respondents rated them. Only two of the ten photos received fewer than three different ripeness levels among the 231 respondents.

FIGURE 2.18 Bananas in various stages of ripeness.

Four of the photos got put into four different categories. And one of the photos was put into each of the five ripeness buckets at least once. The results appear in Figure 2.19 for you to see for yourself.

But this wasn't the point of this fun little informal survey at all. Again, while I think it was interesting that there was that much disparity in categorization, the truth is I was testing something else altogether. I wasn't so much interested in consistency between raters as I was interested in consistency within each rater.

Did you notice the trick? Take a look at the photos again. One of the ten images is exactly same as another one, only it's a mirror image of it. The image of the bunch of bananas that was shown second

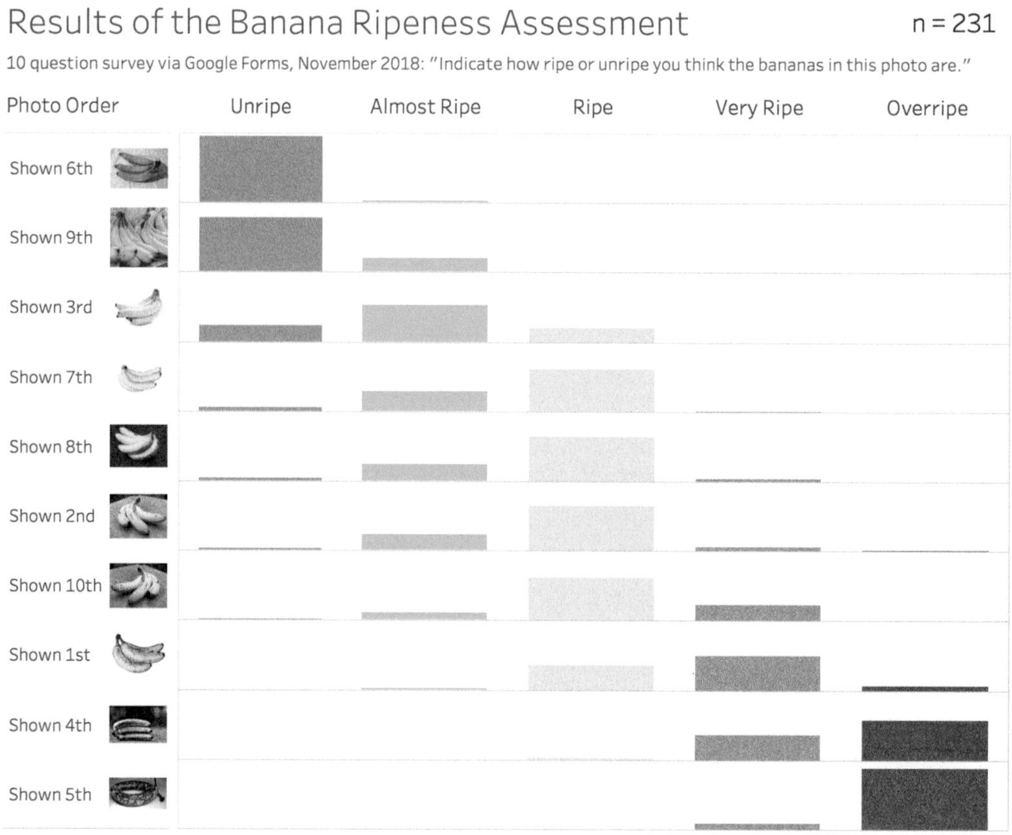

Results of the Banana Ripeness Assessment   n = 231

10 question survey via Google Forms, November 2018: "Indicate how ripe or unripe you think the bananas in this photo are."

FIGURE 2.19   Results of the banana ripeness assessment.

in the survey was shown again at the end of the survey, but it was flipped horizontally. The survey didn't mention anything about this fact, it just simply asked for a ripeness rating for each one.

What I was really interested in finding out was how many people rated these two photos the same, and how many people rated them differently.

My hypothesis was that one in ten or maybe one in twenty would change their rating. In actuality, more than one in three – a full 37% – changed their rating. Of the 231 respondents, 146 rated the tenth photo the same way they rated the second one. But 85 of them rated the photos differently.

This Sankey diagram shows the flow of raters from the way they rated photo 2 on the left to how they rated photo 10 on the right (Figure 2.20).

Another way of looking at the change gives a clue as to what might be happening. If we plot the way respondents rated the second photograph on the rows and the way they rated the tenth photograph on the columns of this five-by-five matrix, we notice that the majority of people who changed their rating increased the level of ripeness.

How respondents changed ripeness rating from photo #2 (left) to #10 (right)

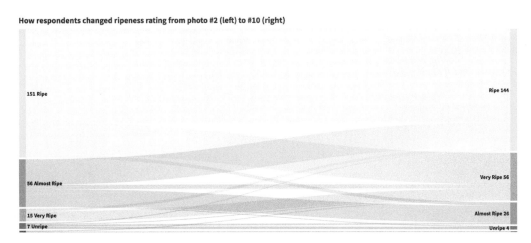

FIGURE 2.20 Respondents' changes in ripeness ratings.

In fact, 77 of the 85 people who changed their rating increased their level of ripeness (e.g. from "almost ripe" to "ripe," or from "ripe" to "very ripe") while only eight decreased their rating (Figure 2.21).

So why did such a high percentage of the raters who changed their rating increase their level of ripeness? Well, let's consider the photo that was shown ninth, the one immediately before the tricky tenth flipped photo (Figure 2.22).

These bananas look a little green, don't they? Now, again, this survey was highly unscientific, informal, and not at all controlled. While it's theoretically possible that respondents could've just been

The 10th photo was a mirror image of the 2nd photo. 37% of respondents give the mirror image a different ripeness level than they gave the original one. See how they changed their rating in the table below.

Gave the same rating — 63%
Gave a different rating — 37%

0   20   40   60   80   100   120   140   160
Number of Respondents

Here's the 10th photo shown in the set, and how respondents rated it based on how they rated the 2nd photo:

Here's the 2nd photo shown in the set, and how respondents rated it, broken down by how they rated the 10th photo:

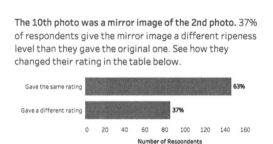

	Unripe	Almost Ripe	Ripe	Very Ripe	Overripe	Total
Unripe	3	2	1	1		7
Almost Ripe	1	20	30	5		56
Ripe		4	110	37		151
Very Ripe			3	12		15
Overripe				1	1	2
	4	26	144	56	1	**231**

FIGURE 2.21   Ratings of photo 2 vs ratings of photo 10.

FIGURE 2.22 The ninth banana photograph shown.

selecting at random to get through it, I don't really have a reason to think that that's what occurred en masse. Respondents weren't offered any incentive or honorarium, so I'll assume for the sake of argument that they gave it a decent shot.

What does it mean, then? To me, it says that it's possible that we're not perfect models of objectivity and consistency when it comes to rating things, that our ratings and opinions have a degree of noise in them, even over short time horizons, and that we're possibly influenced to some degree by the context, or the order in which we provide our opinions.

How is this related to the topic at hand? Every measurement system has some degree of error due to challenges with repeatability and reproducibility. It's true of more than just rating bananas. Your data was created by a measurement system, and that measurement system isn't perfect. Different people performing the measurement process get different results, and even the same person repeating the procedure can end up with different readings sometimes due to sources of noise and error. It's a fact of life that means our data isn't a perfect reflection of reality.

How to Avoid Confusing Data with Reality

Notice that in each of these cases, something in the view of the data itself alerted us to a potential "data-reality gap." Visualizing the data can be one of the best ways to find the gaps.

Earlier in the game, though, it helps to remind ourselves that every data point that exists was collected, stored, accessed, and analyzed via imperfect processes by fallible human beings dealing with equipment that has built-in measurement error.

The more we know about these processes – the equipment used, the protocol followed, the people involved, the steps they took, their motivations – the better equipped we will be to assess the data-reality gap.

Here are seven suggestions to help you avoid confusing data with reality:

- Clearly understand the operational definitions of all metrics.
- Draw the data collection steps as a process flow diagram.
- Understand the limitations and inaccuracies of each step in the process.
- Identify any changes in method or equipment over time.
- Seek to understand the motives of the people collecting and reporting. Could there be any biases or incentives involved?
- Visualize the data and investigate any shifts, outliers, and trends for possible discrepancies.
- Think carefully about data formatting, processing, and transformations.

Ultimately, each data collection activity is unique, and there are too many possible sources of error to list them all. These are some typical ones that I've come across, and you may have your own suggestions.

At the core of the data-reality gap pitfall is our attitude toward data. Do we arrogantly or naively see ourselves as experts on a topic as soon as we get our hands on some data, or do we humbly realize that our knowledge is imperfect, and we may not know the full story?

We can't ever perfectly know the data-reality gap because that would require perfect data. What we can do, though, is seek to identify any gaps that may exist, and take them into account when we use data to shape our understanding of the world we live in.

If the data-reality gap deals with what data is and what it isn't, then the next section seeks to clarify what data can be used for and what it can't be used for.

Pitfall 1D: The Black Swan Pitfall

The way the popular thinking goes, we put data to its best possible use by employing it as a tool to verify truths about the world we live in. And I can see where this idea comes from. I want to know how many bicycles cross the Fremont bridge in a month, so I download the data from the government department website, I carry out a very simple computation, and I come up with my answer.

Bam! Question, meet answer. What could be better than that?

As useful as this information might be to us, there's only one problem with the thinking that affirmative answers are the best thing we can get from data.

It's dead wrong, and it actually plays right into a psychological deficiency we all have as humans.

In fact, the exact opposite is true. The best possible use of data is to teach us what *isn't true* about our previously held conceptions about the world we live in, and to suggest additional questions for which we don't have any answers yet. Embracing this means letting go of our egotistical need to be right all the damn time.

Before explaining, I need to distinguish between two kinds of statements that we deal with when we work with data. In his seminal 1959 work on the epistemology of science, *The Logic of Scientific Discovery*, Austrian-born philosopher Dr. Karl Popper expounded upon these two types of statements: singular statements and universal statements.

- A singular statement (e.g. "That swan over there is white") is a basic observation about the world we live in. It's an empirical fact.
- A universal statement (e.g. "All swans are white") is a hypothesis or theory that divides the world into two kinds of singular statements: those that the universal statement permits, and those that it does not permit. These latter statements that it does not permit, if observed in the real world, would *falsify* the universal statement.

What Popper taught us is that no amount of corroborating observations of singular statements can prove a universal statement to be true. No matter how many white swans we encounter in our search, we haven't come any closer to proving that non-white swans don't exist anywhere in the universe.

But here's the problem: it sure does feel that way. We see nothing but white swans for our entire life. Then we encounter yet another white swan, and our conviction that all swans are white just gets stronger.

It's called induction – arguing from the specific to the general. It's incredibly useful for forming hypotheses to test, but not useful at all for proving those hypotheses true or false. It definitely can give us the feeling of certainty, though, which often leads to very strong convictions.

As Popper pointed out, mere conviction is no basis for accepting a theory into the body of knowledge that's called science. That's faith. There's nothing inherently wrong with faith; we just can't use it to prove something to someone else.

On the other hand, it only takes a single observation of a non-white swan in order to debunk our universal statement and show it to be unequivocally false. That's exactly what happened when, in 1697, Willem de Vlamingh led a group of Dutch explorers to Western Australia and they became the first Europeans to observe a black swan, immediately dispelling the commonly held belief that all swans were white (Figure 2.23).

Like the Europeans and their erroneous induction from repeated observations of white swans to the belief that all swans are white, we often assume that singular statements that we encounter in data verify universal truths. We infer that something we see in the data applies well beyond the time, place, and conditions in which it happened to surface:

FIGURE 2.23   A black swan I photographed on a recent trip to Maui.

- It's not just how many times bikes crossed the Fremont bridge in April 2014, it's how many bikes cross the bridge in general.
- It's not just the preference of certain particular customers, it's the preference of all other potential customers as well.
- It's not just that the pilot manufacturing line had high yields during qualification, it's that the process will also have high yields at full volume production as well.
- It's not just that a particular mutual fund outperformed all others last year, it's that it'll be the best investment going forward.

How often do we come to find out afterward that these inductive leaps from the specific to the general are wrong? It's as if we have a default setting in our brain that assumes that any facts we discover are immutable properties of the universe that will most certainly apply going forward. It's a subtle but insidious mistake in the way we think about data. We even fall into the swan pitfall when there are warning signs right on the prospectus itself: "past performance does not predict future returns."

That's why it's so important that we understand the difference between singular and universal statements, and that any time we consciously decide to work in the realm of universal statements, we commit to construct universal statements that are falsifiable. That is, the set of all possible singular statements that could prove our hypothesis wrong must not be empty. The universal statement "All swans are white" can and was shown to be false. That's a good thing.

But what kind of statement isn't falsifiable? Isn't it theoretically possible to prove anything someone says false? No, not necessarily. Popper pointed out that basic existential statements (e.g. "such-and-such a thing exists.") aren't actually falsifiable. Why not?

Take the singular statement "There exists a black swan." It's pretty easy to show it to be true – all we need to do is to find one. But what if we can't? Have we shown the statement to be false? Actually, no, we haven't, because as much searching as we might've done, there's always the possibility that we missed it, or that it's somewhere we haven't yet looked. Maddening, right?

Pitfall 1E: Falsifiability and the God Pitfall

That's why the statement "God exists" doesn't belong in the realm of science or data analysis. No matter what we do, we can't ever prove it to be false. She/he/it might just be hiding from us, or just not detectable by our senses. That's why it bothers me when people use science or data to try to disprove the existence of a god. It's a pointless exercise, because the hypothesis isn't falsifiable in the first place; it's a basic existential statement. You're welcome to believe it or not. If you don't, just don't delude yourself that you have evidence that one isn't there.

But on the other hand, if you do believe it, don't go spouting a bunch of statements that aren't falsifiable either about how such a god created the universe, and call it "science," because it's not. That's exactly why Judge William Overton ruled that creationism couldn't be taught in schools as science in the 1982 ruling in *McLean v Arkansas Board of Education*. Among other things, the court found that the claims the creationists were making weren't falsifiable, and therefore not science. The Supreme Court agreed with him five years later when a similar case against Louisiana was brought before it.

This is the twofold nature of what I call the "God pitfall" in data analysis – either we form a hypothesis that isn't falsifiable, or we do our best to protect our hypothesis from any possible attempt to show it to be false.

Unlike people who like to get in arguments about religion, do we actively seek to prove our own hypotheses to be false, to debunk our own myths, or do we mostly try to prove ourselves right and others wrong?

If you think about it, we should actually feel *more excited* about data that proves that the universal truths we have adopted are false and in need of updating. It might feel nice when we get corroborating evidence, but the big leaps in our knowledge are made when we realize we've been wrong the whole time. There should be high fives all around when we come across data like this.

If only we were wired that way, but we're just not. Luckily for us, though, those moments of reluctant discovery can be so painful that we never, ever forget them. Reality has a very persistent way of piercing through our delusions time and again.

Because sooner or later our epistemic errors become clear, and we realize that we have fallen into a pitfall yet again.

Avoiding the Swan Pitfall and the God Pitfall

How do we avoid falling into these two epistemic pitfalls? Let's start by considering the process that gets us into trouble. Here's the way that process, and our thinking, often goes:

1. Basic question ➜ 2. Data analysis ➜ 3. Singular statement ➜ {unaware of the inductive leap} ➜ 4. Belief in a universal statement

For example, let's see how that played out in the Fremont Bridge bike counter example:

1. I heard there's a bicycle counter on the Fremont bridge. That's pretty cool, I wonder what I can learn about ridership in my city.
2. Okay, I found some data from the Seattle Department of Transportation, and it looks like …
3. 49,718 **crossed** in the eastbound direction, and 44,859 **crossed** headed west in April 2014.
4. Hmm, so more bicycles **cross** the bridge headed east than west, then. I wonder why that is? Maybe some riders **cross** to get to work in the morning but ride the bus home.

The evidence of the leap can be found in something that might seem insignificant – a verb tense shift. I put the verbs in bold so you'd be more likely to catch it. In step 3 above, we refer to bicycles that "crossed" the bridge (or, as was measured and recorded). But in step 4, we switched from past tense to present tense and used the word "cross." As soon as we did that, we fell prey yet again to the inductive goof.

Instead, I propose we go about things like this:

1. Basic question ➔ 2. Data analysis ➔ 3. Singular statement ➔ 4. Falsifiable universal statement hypothesis ➔ 5. An honest attempt to disprove it

1. How many bicycles cross the Fremont Bridge in a month?

2. Well, I got some data from the Seattle Department of Transportation, and it looks like …

3. The data suggest that the bike counters recorded counts of 49,718 in the eastbound direction, and 44,859 in the westbound direction in April 2014.

4. Hmm, so the counters registered higher counts in the eastbound direction as compared to westbound that month. I wonder whether all months have seen higher counts going east as opposed to west?

5. Let me see whether that's not the case.

A further analysis shows that it is indeed atypical (Figure 2.24).

Okay, so over the past couple years, it looks like my hypothesis was false – counts are typically higher for the westbound ("Fremont Bridge SB") bike counters than for the eastbound ones ("Fremont Bridge NB"), and I can see a seasonal pattern with higher counts in the summer months. I wonder what happened in April 2014, and I'll have to watch the data going forward to see if this seasonal trend holds up, or whether things shift.

Do you see how subtle changes in the way we think about data, and the way we talk about it, result in fewer epistemic errors being made,

Fremont Bridge Bike Counter Measurements

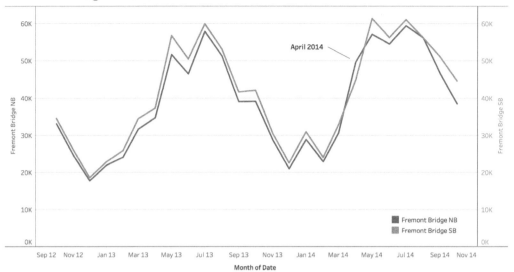

Source: https://data.seattle.gov/Transportation/Fremont-Bridge-Hourly-Bicycle-Counts-by-Month-Octo/65db-xm6k/data

FIGURE 2.24   Fremont Bride bike counter measurements.

better follow-up questions to ask, and a more accurate understanding of the world we live in? Also notice that I took care to avoid falling into the data-reality gap by talking about bike counter counts instead of actual bicycles crossing the bridge.

As always, the devil is in the details. And the devil cares a whole lot about the details about how we think about things.

Chapter Three

Pitfall 2: Technical Trespasses

"All I have to do is work on transition and technique."

—Usain Bolt

How We Process Data

Now that we've had a chance to clear the air about some important philosophical concepts, let's dive into a highly technical part of the data working process that typically happens at the very beginning. Some call it data wrangling; some call it data munging. It's the not-so-glamorous process of getting your data into the proper condition and shape to do the analysis in the first place.

If we compare the data working process to building a house, these data preparation steps are kind of like laying the foundation, and installing the plumbing and the electrical. When it's all said and done, you don't really see any of those things, but if they screwed them up, you're sure not going to want to live there. And working on these parts of the house after people have moved in only gets messier and more difficult.

But this part of the process isn't just critical for the rest of the endeavor; it's also typical for it to take the bulk of the time. An oft-cited figure is that cleaning, structuring, and preparing your data for analysis can account for as much as 50 to 80% of the overall time of the data working project.[1]

So then, identifying and learning to avoid the pitfalls in these critical, time-consuming, and, let's be honest, tedious steps in the process is really important to our success.

Let's start by accepting a few fundamental principles of data wrangling:

- Virtually every data set is dirty and in need of cleaning in some way, shape, or form.
- The transitions are where many of the mistakes happen – reformatting, blending, joining, etc.
- We can learn techniques that will help us avoid forging ahead with dirty data or screwing up the transitions.

If you agree with these principles, then you'll agree that pitfalls abound in the upfront work of preparing data for analysis, but that we can do something about it. As frustrating as these data wrangling issues may be, and as ugly as the process is to deal with them, it can be rewarding to tidy things up, just like that feeling you get when your closet is finally sorted and organized. It's kind of a relief when it's done, no?

Pitfall 2A: The Dirty Data Pitfall

Data is dirty. Let's just get that out there. How is it dirty? In all sorts of ways. Misspelled text values, date format problems, mismatching

---

[1] https://www.nytimes.com/2014/08/18/technology/for-big-data-scientists-hurdle-to-insights-is-janitor-work.html.

units, missing values, null values, incompatible geospatial coordinate formats, the list goes on and on. As ggplot2 creator Hadley Wickham eloquently stated in his book *R for Data Science,* modifying a popular Leo Tolstoy quote, "Tidy datasets are all alike, but every messy dataset is messy in its own way."[2]

Open data that you can download for free on the web from government departments can be particularly filthy. Let's take a fun data set to work with: car tow data. The Baltimore City Department of Transportation provides a downloadable record of over 61,300 car tow events dating from January 2017 back to October 2012.[3] Figure 3.1 shows what the first 11 columns of the earliest tow events look like.

As the software marketers would have us believe, we can quickly connect to our data and presto! Just like that, we can drag and drop our way to answers and powerful insights in our data. Sounds promising, doesn't it? Let's try it out. Every vehicle was manufactured in a particular year, and the good folks at the tow yards have done us the fabulous favor of capturing this attribute for us in the data. I'd like to know the typical year of manufacture of cars towed in Baltimore, so I simply compute the average vehicle year and round to the nearest integer and I get . . . 23?

Hmm, that seems strange. It surely can't mean 1923, and clearly 2023 isn't possible, unless maybe they're all DeLoreans. What's going on here? How can the average vehicle year be 23?

Let's look more closely, as we so often have to do with data. We don't actually have to look too closely at this data set to start to figure out that something happened in the processing of vehicle year from the tow yard to the form to the digital record.

Even just a quick glance at the column for vehicle Year in the spreadsheet itself shows us we're in for some serious trouble with this attribute. The very first value is 99, which is presumably 1999.

---

[2] https://r4ds.had.co.nz/tidy-data.html.
[3] https://data.baltimorecity.gov/Transportation/DOT-Towing/k78j-azhn.

	A	B	C	D	E	F	G	H	I	J	K
1	propertynumber	towedDateTime	vehicleType	vehicleYear	vehicleMake	vehicleModel	vehicleColor	tagNumber	towCompany	towCharge	towedFromLocation
2	P206813	10/23/10 10:50	Car	99	Mercedes	C230	Burg	7EVM54	Jim Elliotts Towing	$140.00	200 Longwood Rd
3	P206814	10/23/10 11:00	Car	91	Lexus	LS400	Gray	EXV9405	Bermans Towing	$140.00	700 W Fayette St
4	P206815	10/23/10 11:35	Car	4	Chevrolet	Cavalier	Blue	9ERW87	Frankford Towing	$130.00	500 Grundy St
5	P206816	10/23/10 12:04	Scooter	8	Velocity		Black		Bermans Towing	$140.00	2100 North Ave
6	F011135	10/24/10 12:38	Van		LEXUS			9GAA97	City	$130.00	U/B W HUGHES ST.
7	P206905	10/25/10 11:12	SUV	6	Toyota	RAV4	Blue	410M804	Cherryhill Towing Service	$140.00	200 Fredhilton Pass
8	P206914	10/25/10 14:49	Car	97	Hyundai	Tiburon	Red	8EEZ91	City	$140.00	1 N Paca St
9	P207054	10/25/10 14:53	Car	95	Honda	Accord	Burgundy	A219155	Fallsway	$140.00	600 N Caroline St
10	P209809	12/20/10 8:41	SUV	0	Jeep	Cherokee	White	27415M5	Fallsway	$130.00	200 Monroe St
11	P209807	12/20/10 16:45	Car	93	Honda	Accord	Brown	4ELS75	Fallsway	$130.00	1400 E Monument St
12	P209808	12/21/10 7:37	Car	95	Bmw	318I	White	4EDT18	Fallsway	$130.00	100 S Greene St
13	P209775	12/22/10 12:35	Car	98	Pontaic	Grand Prix	Red	3FSH05	City	$130.00	3719 Greenmount Ave
14	P209776	12/22/10 12:41	Car	0	Nissan	Maxima	Black	9GCD55	Bermans Towing	$140.00	1400 Russell St
15	P209777	12/22/10 12:45	Van	97	Mercury	Villager	Green		Bermans Towing	$140.00	500 N Carey St
16	P209778	12/22/10 13:10	Car	93	Mitsubishi	Diamante	Silver		Aarons Automotive Services	$130.00	900 E 22nd St
17	P209779	12/22/10 13:26	Pick-up Truc	3	Ford	F350	Black	83S213	Aarons Automotive Services	$130.00	2100 N Wolfe St
18	P209780	12/22/10 13:30	Van	99	Chevrolet	Astro	White		City	$130.00	2000 Ellsworth St
19	P209781	12/22/10 13:37	Car	0	Dodge	Stratus	Silver	9FJC68	Frankford Towing	$130.00	1500 E Belvedere Ave
20	P209782	12/22/10 14:15	Pick-up Truc	91	Ford	F150	Red/Silver	48X235	City	$130.00	200 S Ellwood Ave
21	P209783	12/22/10 14:26	Car	98	Honda	Accord	Black	9AC4902	Aarons Automotive Services	$130.00	2800 Harford Rd
22	P209785	12/22/10 14:36	Car	98	Buick	Lesabre	Tan	7AA3187	City	$140.00	1600 Gwynn Falls Parkway
23	P209786	12/22/10 14:38	Car	99	Ford	Taurus	Black	7AD3025	Frankford Towing	$130.00	500 N Luzerne
24	P209788	12/22/10 14:40	Trailer	?	Ez Loader	Hydra-Sports	Silver	AA67474	City	$130.00	4020 Belle Ave
25	P209784	12/22/10 14:40	Boat	75	Sportcraft	Caprice	White	1703PN	City	$130.00	4020 Belle Ave
26	P209787	12/22/10 16:57	SUV	5	Lexus	RX330	Silver	33742CB	Frankford Towing	$130.00	3000 Mayfield

FIGURE 3.1 Baltimore City Department of Transportation tow records.

The next value is 91, and we're comfortable that we can assume this car's year is most likely 1991. But what about the value in the third row – 4? My best guess is that this represents 2004. Also, there's a blank cell as well as a "?" farther down in this same column – does this mean in the first case the person recording the tow purposefully left it blank while in the latter they just didn't know the vehicle year? There could be more than one meaning for these values.

Let's stop for a second and think about the process involved in collecting and storing this data. When's the last time you had your car towed? I needed a tow the week prior to writing this very sentence after an unfortunate fender bender close to my home in Bellevue, Washington. I stood out in the rain and the dark in the middle of the road and waited for the police officer and the tow truck operator to complete the soggy paperwork and decide who got which carbon copy. Presumably data is created from forms that were produced in moments just like this. When my tow truck driver asked me for my vehicle year, I'm pretty sure I told him it was a 2011, but I didn't see whether he wrote down "2011," "11," or maybe "'11" with an apostrophe in front of the first digit. And I have no idea who keyed this information into a computer, or what software was used to generate the form they filled out required in this field. Much is lost in translation, and evidently some people missed the Y2K memo a couple decades ago.

But without a doubt, we can have some sympathy for the tow truck drivers and the data entry clerks at the tow yard. If I had to type in over 61,000 rows like this, I'd probably get a lot of them wrong, too. So what are we going to do about this messy quantitative field telling us the year of the vehicle that was towed? Let's visualize it using a histogram (Figure 3.2).

We can clearly see that there are two groups, and that it appears at first glance that there is nothing in between them. The first group on the left has vehicle year values between 0 and 17. We can guess that these are cars built between 2000 and 2017. The second group has vehicle year values between 82 and 99. These were most likely built between 1982 and 1999. We can adjust the vehicle years by adding 2000 to vehicle years between 0 and 17 and 1900 to years greater than that.

Original Vehicle Year

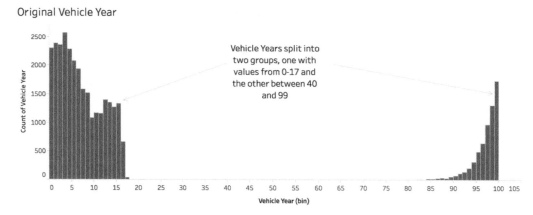

FIGURE 3.2 The raw vehicle year data visualized in a histogram.

The corrected histogram looks like Figure 3.3.

This looks much better! We're done, right? Not so fast. Often, the first adjustment or correction is a course adjustment, but more fine-tuning is needed. We can mop the floor, but sometimes we need to go back and use a spot cleaner on a tough blemish. This data set still has some of those.

We can see that the corrected vehicle year histogram has a very long tail to the left. It looks like there's nothing there, but there

Corrected Vehicle Year: Add 2000 to Years 0-17 and add 1900 to all other years

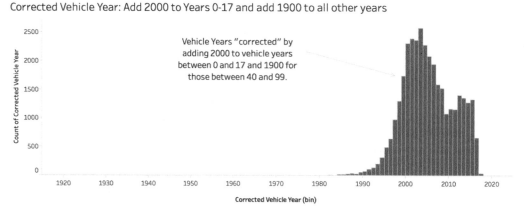

FIGURE 3.3 The adjusted vehicle year data visualized in a histogram.

are actually really short bars for individual values at 1920 (originally 20), 1940 (originally 40), 1960 (originally 60), and 1963 (originally 63). Are these really old cars that got towed? Let's see what they are in Figure 3.4.

Now, we can be pretty sure that the "Toyota Camray" (sic) is actually a Toyota Camry, and there's no way it was made in 1920, because Toyota didn't start making this model until 1982.[4] The Volvo S40 definitely isn't from 1940, but we can guess why an S40 would have a "40" entered in this field. The Jeep Liberty couldn't possibly be from 1960, because Jeep only made this model between 2002 and 2012.[5] The 1963 "Cadillac Sedan Deville" could very well be a 1963 Cadillac Sedan de Ville, so we'll assume that value is correct.

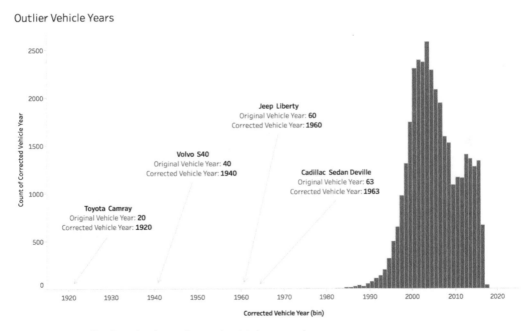

FIGURE 3.4 Outliers in the adjusted vehicle year data.

---

[4] https://en.wikipedia.org/wiki/Toyota_Camry.
[5] https://en.wikipedia.org/wiki/Jeep_Liberty.

So now what do we do with the other three that are clearly erroneous vehicle year values? Do we filter them out? Do we do more research and find out what model year they actually are? Do we just leave them alone as they are?

That largely depends on the analysis we need to do, and whether these values can make a big difference on our findings. As we'll discuss later, outlier values can have a large impact on the average (arithmetic mean), so we should be deliberate about our choice, and we should leave detailed notes about any adjustments we make, or any clearly erroneous values that we leave in the view for our audience.

As it is, I'll leave those four questionable values in the data set, and I'll recalculate the average vehicle year to be 2005, rounded to the nearest integer. That seems like it makes a lot more sense than 23, doesn't it? Removing those four outliers only changes the computed average by one thousandth of a year, and it is completely washed out in the rounding to the nearest integer. So I feel fine leaving them in for my analysis, even though I'm pretty sure they're wrong. They don't materially affect the insight I glean.

Speaking of this insight, what does the average vehicle year really tell us here? I presented this data to a class of data science students at the for-profit education company Metis in Seattle earlier this year. One very bright student pointed out that while the statistic 2005 is interesting, it's slightly misleading, because the set of possible vehicle years isn't constant over the time. You can't tow a 2017 Buick in 2014. So it's more meaningful to obtain an average vehicle year *within* each tow year, and then track how this average changes as time goes along. We'll have more to say about averages in the coming chapters.

Let's talk more about that "Camray" though. This misspelling gives us a window into another dirty aspect of this data set, the Vehicle Make field. We'll start with this field, because in theory that should be much more limited in its range of values than the Vehicle Model field. Most makes (e.g. Honda) have many models (Civic, Accord, etc.)

It turns out there are actually 899 distinct entries in the Vehicle Make field in our data set. Figure 3.5 shows the top 100, ranked (and sized) by the total number of entries (tow events) in the data set.

We can quickly identify vehicle makes that we would expect to see: Chevrolet, Toyota, Honda, Dodge, Ford, Acura. But we also see Chevy, and even "Cheverolet" and "Chevolet." We see "MAZDA," and even "Mazada." We see "1," and also "Unknown." Uh-oh, there's Hyundai, which is fine, but there's also "Hyundia."

And the word cloud only shows the top 100 most towed makes. There are still 799 more to go! In the overall list, we find Dodge, but also "Dode," "Dodg," "Dodg3e," "Dodgfe," "Dfdge," "Dpdge," and so on. And don't get me started with all the other permutations of "Chevrolet." One of my favorites, though, is "Peterbutt." I got a chuckle out of this misspelling of "Peterbilt." You also have to get a kick out of "Mitsubishit" making an appearance in the list.

But seriously, what the heck are we supposed to do with such a huge mess? How could we ever know which was the most common vehicle make reportedly towed during that time range?

FIGURE 3.5 This word cloud gives a general sense of which vehicle makes were most often towed.

OpenRefine[6] is a helpful tool that can be downloaded for free and used to identify and quickly combine similar values in a column, among other handy things. If we open the data set in OpenRefine and carry out a cluster function on the Vehicle Make field, choosing a key collision method with an ngram-fingerprint keying function and ngram size of 1, we can get a quick sense of just how many erroneous values there are for each vehicle make (Figure 3.6).

This specific algorithm has found 113 different clusters to merge, and we can review them one by one as we scroll down the page. I highly recommend doing this, because when we do, we see that the algorithm isn't perfect. For example, it wants to create a cluster for both "Dodger" and "Dodge," and it suggests merging "Suzuui" (clearly a misspelling of "Suzuki") into the Isuzu cluster (Figure 3.7).

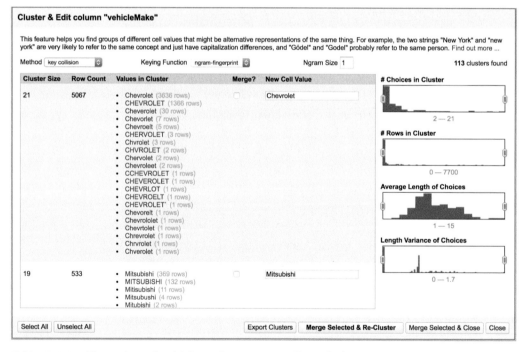

FIGURE 3.6   Clustering of vehicle make names in OpenRefine.

---

[6] http://openrefine.org/.

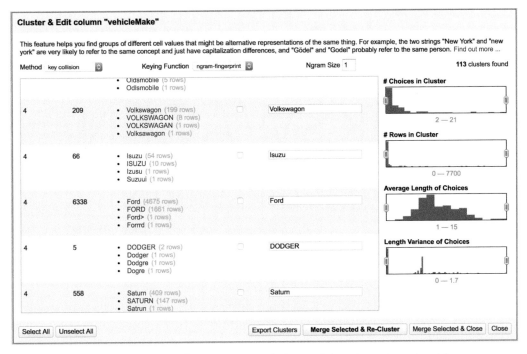

FIGURE 3.7 Imperfections in the recommendations of the clustering algorithm.

We also notice also in Figure 3.7 that Open Refine has suggested that we create a distinct cluster for "Volkswagon," right? If you're thinking there's nothing wrong with that, as I first did, you'd miss the fact that the four different values in this group are all misspellings of "Volkswagen," which is the correct spelling. If we scroll, we'd find that the algorithm suggested a separate group for this correct spelling, which we can correct. If we do, we'll find that there are 36 different ways Volkswagen was spelled in the data set (Figure 3.8).

When we use the ngram-fingerprint algorithm and do a quick search for obvious misses, we can effectively reduce the count of distinct values in the Vehicle Make field from 899 to just 507. That's a huge reduction in complexity. But are we done?

We can continue to try different clustering methods – if we run a nearest neighbor Levenshtein algorithm we can further reduce the distinct number of values to 473. Finally, we can review each of these

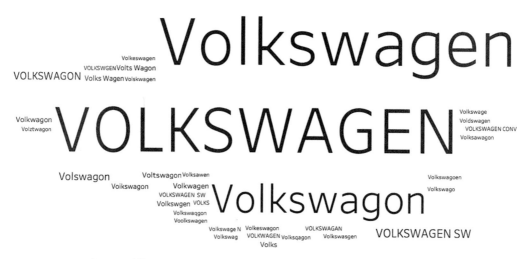

FIGURE 3.8   The 36 different ways Volkswagen was spelled in the data set.

473 values and look at them one by one, adjusting them by editing each value that didn't get picked up in the clusters, which effectively finds and replaces all instances of the erroneous values. For example, neither of these algorithms decided the two records having the vehicle make "Acira" should belong with the "Acura" group, so I went ahead and manually changed them myself (Figure 3.9).

This is time-consuming stuff, but imagine how much more painful it would be if we had to sift through all 899 distinct values for the Vehicle Make field. At least the clustering algorithms knock the number down to about half.

After about half an hour of going through the list and manually fixing a number of obviously incorrect entries that didn't get grouped with the others using the clustering algorithms, I ended up with 336 total distinct values for Vehicle Make. Note that I still ended up with interesting entries like "Burnt Car," "Pete," "Rocket," and a whole host of numbers in this field, so it's not perfect. But that field is a whole lot less dirty than when I started.

But so what? Was it worth it? How did it affect our analysis? Let's take a look at the before-and-after analysis of top Vehicle Makes by number of tow events in Figure 3.10.

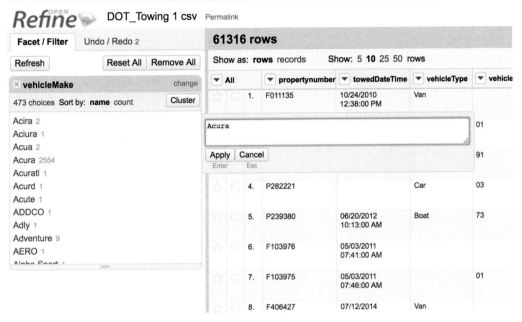

FIGURE 3.9   Editing the data values one by one that the clustering algorithm didn't catch.

Notice that the top two vehicle makes, Honda and Ford, are still in the top two spots, but have increased by 2,454 (+46%) and 1,685 tows (+36%), respectively. Their position in the list may not have changed, but those are some significant jumps in value.

And not all makes remained in the same spot on the ranking list. Toyota moved from the fourth spot up to the third spot, and Chevrolet dropped from 3rd to 4th in rank. Both also increased in count by a few thousand. Notably, Jeep jumped from 15th to 10th, and Volkswagen, which wasn't even in the top 25 originally, ends up in the 11th spot after our clustering, merging, and cleaning effort.

So yes, the effort to clean up the dirty data field results in a material change to our analysis. We would've had some serious misconceptions about which vehicles were towed the most, and how often the most common vehicle makes were reportedly towed by Baltimore DOT during this time period.

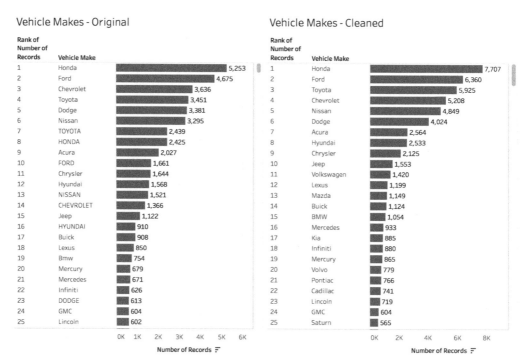

FIGURE 3.10   Before and after: analysis of vehicle make frequencies before cleaning and after.

So cleaning the data, at least to the degree that we cleaned it, mattered in the end.

How Do We Know When Our Data Is Clean Enough?

But when is a given data set clean enough? Like a kitchen countertop, it can always be cleaner. We hit a point of diminishing returns in our preparation of any data set, though, where more elbow grease and scrubbing doesn't yield sufficient incremental benefit to warrant the time and effort.

Where is that point? How do we know when we've arrived? Of course it depends on the sensitivity and criticality of the decisions and the tasks our analysis will inform. Are we landing a rover on Mars? Okay, that's one thing. But what if you don't need that level of precision?

Let's stick with the Baltimore vehicle towing example, and consider a fictional scenario. Say you're Vince, and you run Vince's Auto Body & Paint Shop, which happens to be right next to one of the two tow yards. You've been noticing that owners of cars that get towed are coming to you for paint touch-up after they claim their vehicles from the yard. You're thinking of running a promotion to attract more business of that type, and you want to make sure you have enough of the right kind of paint.

You get the data and look at the vehicle color breakdown. Here's what you see (Figure 3.11).

You have a pretty good sense, now, of the main colors of cars, but is it good enough for your buyers to start placing orders? How can we summarize what we know so far?

- 70.1% of the records reportedly are cars with one of 17 main color values: Black, Silver, White, Blue, and so on.

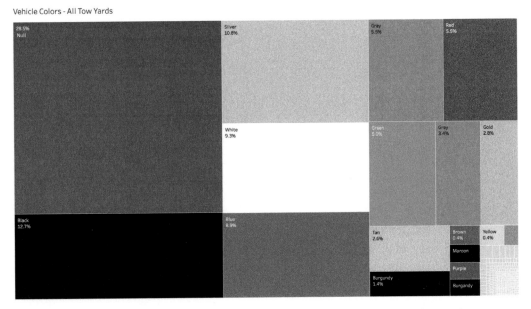

FIGURE 3.11 A treemap of vehicle colors based on towing records to the yards.

- 28.5% of the records don't have any color indicated at all – the field is blank, or null.
- The final 1.4% are records associated with 360 different values in the vehicle color field.
  - ◆ A quick glance indicates that this 1.4% includes both unusual colors such as Beige and Navy, but also alternative values of the main colors, like "black" with a lower case "b," as well as mis-spellings such as "Greeen" and "Clack," among many others.

What do you do? The data is dirty, sure, but is it dirty enough? Should you spend any time on this at all? Well, a few things are relatively easy to do. Merging "Gray" and "Grey" into one category, and also "Burgandy" and "Burgundy" seem like useful steps that don't take much time and would affect your paint supply orders somewhat. The top 17 colors are actually just 15 colors, after all. That wasn't too hard. That was like wiping the big coffee spill off the kitchen counter.

The next big issue to address is the fact that there are so many null values. You can do a few things here. You can just filter them out and go with the resulting percentages. That would basically be assuming that the null group is filled with vehicles that have the exact same color breakdown as the non-null records. Might not be a horrible assumption, given your level of required precision.

But with a little extra digging, you find that you're in luck! Almost all of the null values – 17,123 out of 17,491 – are actually associated with the *other* tow yard across town. The folks at the tow yard next to your shop are much more diligent about capturing vehicle color – only 368 of the 44,193 records at your location have null color val-ues. So nulls really aren't much of a problem at all for you after all. You've been dealt a get-out-of-dirty-data-jail-free card (this time).

Here's what the color breakdown of *your* target customers looks like (Figure 3.12).

Null now accounts for only 0.8% of the filtered records, and the "Other" bucket accounts for 1.9%. If "Other" were a paint color, it

Vehicle Colors - Pulaski Tow Yard

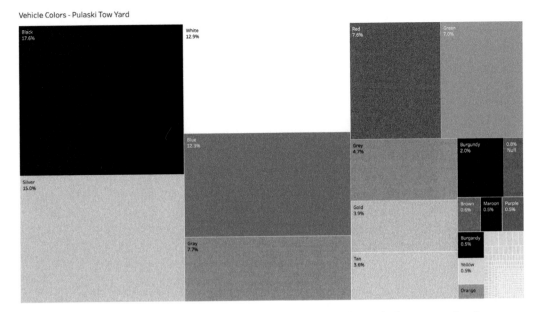

FIGURE 3.12   A treemap of records of towed vehicles to the Pulaski tow yard only.

would be the eleventh most common color – not even in the top 10. In other words, you have a pretty good handle on 97.3% of the potential demand, provided good records were kept, and as long as color frequency in the near future matches what has been. That's probably good enough to roll with, right?

Time out. We still have a few colors spelled different ways in the top 15, and the entire data set is still case sensitive. We need to fix that, and it should be easy enough to do.

Let's write a quick calculation to do the following (Figure 3.13):

- Convert both "Grey" and "grey" to "gray."
- Convert both "Burgandy" and "burgandy" to "burgundy."
- Convert all text values to lowercase (e.g. merge "Blue" and "blue," "Red" and "red," etc.).

Once we create this new corrected vehicle color field, we can update our treemap and filter out the null values as well as all records with

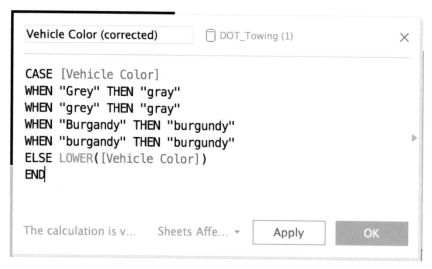

FIGURE 3.13 A calculated field in Tableau to correct for a few known discrepancies in the color field.

color field values not included in the top 15. Figure 3.14 is our final output that we send to our buyers for coordination of inventory and orders with our paint vendors ahead of the promotion to the tow yard customers.

That was probably a good balance of relatively simple and speedy data cleaning steps with an updated analysis that gives us that extra bit of confidence in our findings. Recall that our initial analysis yielded the following skewed "insight":

- Q: What percentage of all recorded vehicles towed during the time period had a color value of "Gray"?
- A: 5.5%

If we ran with this, we'd have dramatically underordered gray paint, which actually accounted for about one-eighth of all recorded vehicle colors at the tow yard next to us. We can take another pass using Tableau Prep, and use the pronunciation algorithm to catch some of the rarer misspellings of vehicle color as shown in Figure 3.15.

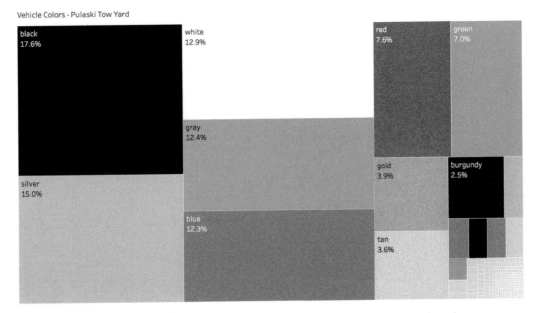

Vehicle Colors - Pulaski Tow Yard

FIGURE 3.14 The final treemap of known, non-null vehicle colors towed to the Pulaski yard.

We see that there aren't quite 50 misspellings of gray; there are only 17, including "Greyu," "Grety," "Greyw," "Greyy," "Frey," and our good friend "Gary." This wasn't difficult, thanks to the magic of algorithms and software, but did our analysis change materially based on our more rigorous cleaning operation? Here's the new treemap we produced after the second pass of cleaning color names using Tableau Prep (Figure 3.16).

We added a second digit to interrogate further, but it doesn't seem like the proportions have changed significantly. Gray increases from 12.4% to 12.54%. Not a huge jump, and probably not enough to affect our order quantities. Performing this more detailed cleaning operation certainly didn't hurt, and it was simple enough, but we would've probably been okay with the coarser cleaning operation in our first pass.

But how were we supposed to know ahead of time if the second pass would've mattered? The key is to consider the "Other"

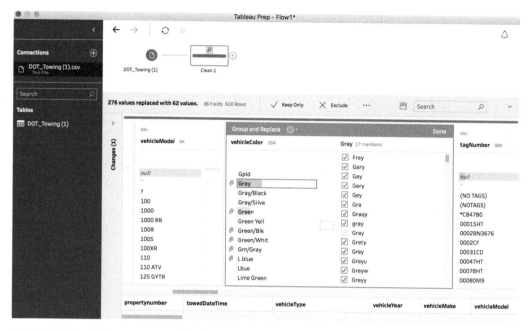

FIGURE 3.15   Cleaning car colors further.

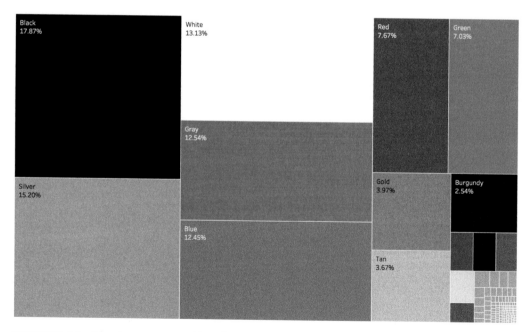

FIGURE 3.16   The treemap resulting from our second cleaning pass using Tableau Prep.

bucket, the dirty values "in the weeds" – those in the bottom of the pareto chart. In our case, we're talking about the 360 values in the vehicle color field that make up the bottom 1.9% of records. Is this group large enough for our particular task that we really need to crack into it, or would we be fine if they magically all happened to be the exact same value? Like everything in life, there's the horrible, there's the impeccable, and, somewhere in between, there's good enough.

Thank goodness for that.

Pitfall 2B: Bad Blends and Joins

As we've seen, dirty data can be challenging to face when working with just one data set all by itself. It can be even more of a headache when bringing more than one data set together into the same analysis. Whether we're working with SQL joins, merging or appending data in an analytics tool like Tableau or Power BI, or working with an old familiar friend, the VLOOKUP function in Excel, we're stepping onto a portion of the path with some treacherous pitfalls. Let's see what can happen.

Now let's say you're Allison, a marketing director at a consumer products company. You want to grow your website so that you can position your company's product as a global leader in its category. You want to understand where your web traffic came from in 2016, so you use Google Analytics to create a map of Pageviews of your site (Figure 3.17).

This is really helpful, and it tells you that the bulk of your traffic is coming from the United States, India, the UK, Canada, and Australia. But you want to dig a little deeper. You'd like to compare the amount of traffic to your site in 2016 with the population of each country in 2016. Are there some countries with really high traffic compared to how many people live there? Or on the other hand, those where the traffic doesn't seem to match up with the opportunity based on population alone?

FIGURE 3.17   A world map of 2016 Pageviews of Allison's company website.

To do that, you'll need to bring another data set into the analysis – one that gives you population for each country in your Google Analytics data. You find a World Bank web page[7] that lets you download 2016 country population as an Excel file or CSV, and you also stumble across a page on Wikipedia[8] that lists the population of sovereign states and dependent territories based on projections published by the United Nations. Could one of these do the trick?

You decide to consider each of these lists independently. First, the list in Google Analytics that you've just mapped includes 180 distinct values. In comparison, the World Bank population Excel file contains 228 distinct values. You can tell that part of the reason the World Bank list is larger is that it also includes values that group countries together like "World," "North America," and "High income." So some rows aren't individual countries at all. The Wikipedia list, which also includes dependent territories such as the Cook Islands and Guam, contains 234 distinct values – it's the largest of the three. (See Figure 3.18.)

---

[7] https://data.worldbank.org/data-catalog/Population-ranking-table.
[8] https://en.wikipedia.org/wiki/List_of_countries_by_population_(United_Nations).

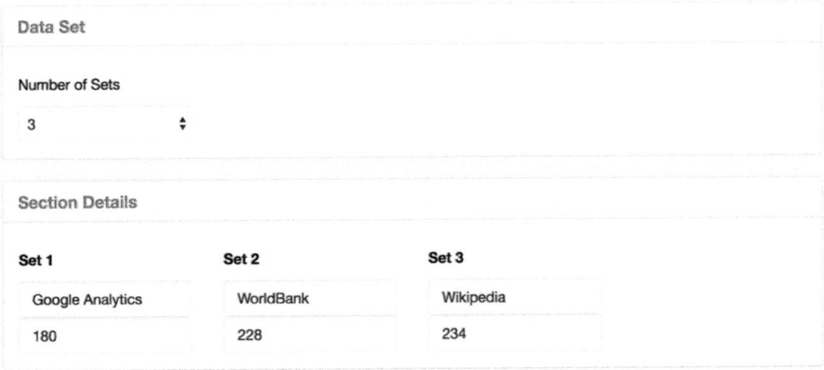

Data Set		
Number of Sets		
3 ‡		

Section Details		
Set 1	**Set 2**	**Set 3**
Google Analytics	WorldBank	Wikipedia
180	228	234

FIGURE 3.18 An overview of the number of distinct country names in three different data sets.

So there's clearly not a 1:1:1 match in the respective country name lists between these different data sources. A quick exploration of the total number of distinct values in each list is a helpful step to get an idea of what you're working with, but it doesn't tell you the whole story. You decide to match up the Google Analytics list with each list independently to get a sense of whether your analysis will be complete.

First, when you consider how the Google Analytics list compares with the World Bank population list, you notice that there are 82 string values in the World Bank field list that aren't included in the Google Analytics country list. But since this list includes a number of grouped values, and since Google Analytics is your primary source for traffic data, you're not as concerned with these as you are with the 34 countries in Google Analytics that aren't included in the World Bank list.

Google Analytics has 34 unmatched values, the two lists have 146 in common, and the World Bank has 82 unmatched values, yielding the Venn diagram in Figure 3.19 and the list of 34 countries unique to Google Analytics:

Instead of "St. Kitts & Nevis," the World Bank has the entry "St. Kitts and Nevis." Instead of "Bahamas," the World Bank uses

WorldBank List	Google Analytics List	Pageviews
Null	Antigua & Barbuda	27
	Bahamas	11,881
	Bosnia & Herzegovina	14,400
	Brunei	2,618
	Cape Verde	3,978
	Congo - Brazzaville	817
	Congo - Kinshasa	1,305
	Côte d'Ivoire	2,067
	Czechia	88,218
	Egypt	54,916
	Eritrea	457
	Gambia	330
	Guernsey	694
	Hong Kong	238,493
	Iran	53,667
	Jersey	589
	Kyrgyzstan	212
	Laos	1,627
	Macau	3,959
	Macedonia (FYROM)	4,386
	Martinique	2,043
	Myanmar (Burma)	21,493
	Palestine	1,506
	Réunion	6,170
	Russia	315,740
	Slovakia	34,755
	South Korea	313,568
	St. Kitts & Nevis	477
	Syria	771
	Taiwan	460,819
	Trinidad & Tobago	12,554
	U.S. Virgin Islands	175
	Venezuela	27,805
	Yemen	6,867

FIGURE 3.19 A Venn diagram showing overlap between Google Analytics and World Bank.

"Bahamas, The." Instead of "U.S. Virgin Islands," they list "Virgin Islands (U.S.)." Rather than "Hong Kong," the World Bank gives us population figures for "Hong Kong SAR, China." While Google Analytics includes Pageview data for "Taiwan," the World Bank has no entry at all for this part of the world, presumably due to the fact that China often seeks to reign in any organization that refers to this island as a sovereign nation.

The fact that there are mismatches, missing values, and small differences in the strings used to indicate various countries means that there's a risk that you'll miss them in your analysis. Why?

If you were to do an inner join on this field in SQL, where you only keep records with country values in common (the overlapping area of the two circles in the Venn diagram in Figure 3.19), then these 34 countries would be left out of the resulting table. Even if you do a left-outer join, or alternatively a VLOOKUP in Excel, in which you keep both the overlapping records as well as any that are unique to Google Analytics, the population value for these 34 countries will be empty, null, because there is no exact match in the World Bank data set.

Would it matter? It depends. Here's the pageview per thousand inhabitants analysis using the original World Bank data set (on the left) and using a cleaned version (on the right), where the country names were made to match and the population of Taiwan was added (Figure 3.20).

Did it make a difference? Three of the top 25 countries in terms of views per thousand people would have been missing from your analysis if you didn't take into account the mismatching values in the country field.

Next, you do a similar comparison of the Google Analytics list and the Wikipedia list, and find that Google Analytics has 16 unmatched values, the two have 164 in common, and Wikipedia has 70 unmatched values (Figure 3.21).

Just for fun, you compare all three, and discover that there are 145 country names that appear in all three lists (Figure 3.22).

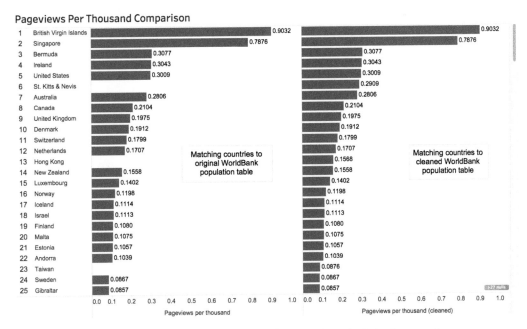

Pageviews Per Thousand Comparison

#	Country	Original	Cleaned
1	British Virgin Islands	0.9032	0.9032
2	Singapore	0.7876	0.7876
3	Bermuda	0.3077	0.3077
4	Ireland	0.3043	0.3043
5	United States	0.3009	0.3009
6	St. Kitts & Nevis		0.2909
7	Australia	0.2806	0.2806
8	Canada	0.2104	0.2104
9	United Kingdom	0.1975	0.1975
10	Denmark	0.1912	0.1912
11	Switzerland	0.1799	0.1799
12	Netherlands	0.1707	0.1707
13	Hong Kong		0.1568
14	New Zealand	0.1558	0.1558
15	Luxembourg	0.1402	0.1402
16	Norway	0.1198	0.1198
17	Iceland	0.1114	0.1114
18	Israel	0.1113	0.1113
19	Finland	0.1080	0.1080
20	Malta	0.1075	0.1075
21	Estonia	0.1057	0.1057
22	Andorra	0.1039	0.1039
23	Taiwan		0.0876
24	Sweden	0.0867	0.0867
25	Gibraltar	0.0857	0.0857

Matching countries to original WorldBank population table

Matching countries to cleaned WorldBank population table

Pageviews per thousand

Pageviews per thousand (cleaned)

FIGURE 3.20 Comparison of pageviews per thousand analysis before and after cleaning.

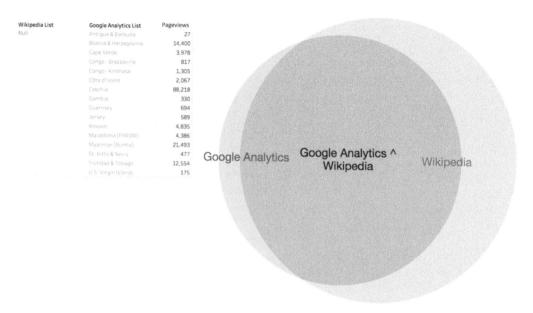

Wikipedia List	Google Analytics List	Pageviews
Null	Antigua & Barbuda	27
	Bosnia & Herzegovina	14,400
	Cape Verde	3,978
	Congo - Brazzaville	817
	Congo - Kinshasa	1,305
	Côte d'Ivoire	2,067
	Czechia	88,218
	Gambia	330
	Guernsey	694
	Jersey	589
	Kosovo	4,835
	Macedonia (FYROM)	4,386
	Myanmar (Burma)	21,493
	St. Kitts & Nevis	477
	Trinidad & Tobago	12,554
	U.S. Virgin Islands	175

FIGURE 3.21   A Venn diagram showing overlap between Google Analytics and the Wikipedia population list.

Overlap between Country Name Lists

FIGURE 3.22   A Venn diagram comparing all three country name lists.

So you decide that the Wikipedia list is a better match with your original Google Analytics data set because it has more records in common, and you only have to adjust 16 values to get them to line up perfectly. That's not so bad, so you find and replace those 16 values in the data set you have created from the Wikipedia page and get to work.

This has been a successful story, so far. Allison has avoided the common pitfall of bringing together two data sets and doing calculations and analysis of the two merged tables without first considering the areas of overlap and lack thereof.

A technicality? Sure, but that's exactly why it's called a technical trespass.

Chapter Four

Pitfall 3: Mathematical Miscues

"Calculation never made a hero."

—*John Henry Newman*

How We Calculate Data

There are heroes and there are goats. As the epigraph states, calculation may have "never made a hero" – a status more commonly attributed to women and men who pull off daring acts of bravado in spite of great odds – but failure to calculate properly has definitely made more than one goat.

Infamous examples abound, such as the disintegration of the Mars Climate Orbiter[1] on September 23, 1999, due to atmospheric stresses resulting from a problematic trajectory that brought it too

---

[1] https://en.wikipedia.org/wiki/Mars_Climate_Orbiter.

close to the red planet. The root cause of the faulty trajectory? A piece of software provided by Lockheed Martin calculated impulse from thruster firing in non-SI pound-force seconds while a second piece of software provided by NASA read that result, expecting it to be in Newton seconds per the specification. One pound-force is equivalent to 4.45 Newtons, so the calculation was off by quite a bit.

These cases remind us that to err truly is human. And also that it can be really easy to get the math wrong. It's a pitfall we fall into so often.

We make calculations any time we apply mathematical processes to our data. Some basic examples include:

- Summing quantities to various levels of aggregation, such as buckets of time – the amount of some quantity per week, or month, or year
- Dividing quantities in our data with other quantities in our data to produce rates or ratios
- Working with proportions or percentages
- Converting from one unit of measure to another

If you feel like these basic types of calculations are so simple that they're sure to be free from errors, you're wrong. I've fallen into these data pitfalls on many occasions, and I've seen others fall into them time and time again. I'm sure you have seen it, too. We'll save more advanced computations for later chapters. Let's just start with the basics and work up from there.

Pitfall 3A: Aggravating Aggregations

We aggregate data when we group records that have an attribute in common. There are all kinds of such groupings that we deal with in our world. Sometimes groups in our data form a hierarchy. Here are just a handful:

- Time: hour, day, week, month, year
- Geography: city, county, state, country
- Organization: employee, team, department, company

- Sports: team, division, conference, league
- Product: SKU, product type, category, brand

Whether we're reporting sales at various levels or tallying votes for an election, these aggregation calculations can be critical to our success. Let's consider an example from the world of aviation.

The U.S. Federal Aviation Administration allows pilots to voluntarily report instances where their aircraft strikes wildlife during takeoff, flight, approach, or landing.[2] I know, gruesome, and pretty scary from the point of view of the pilot, the passengers, and especially the poor critter. They also provide the data to the public, so we can have a sense of what's going on.

Let's say we got our hands on a particular extract from these records, and we wanted to know how the reported number of wildlife strikes has been changing over time, if at all. We create a timeline (Figure 4.1) of recorded strikes, by year.

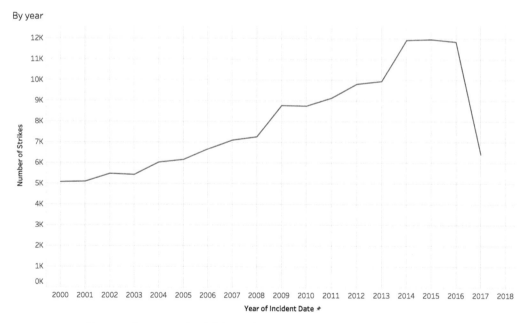

FIGURE 4.1   Count of reported wildlife strikes by aircraft in the U.S., by year.

_____

[2] https://wildlife.faa.gov/.

We can see from this timeline that there are records in our extract going as far back as 2000. It seems to indicate an increasing trend in reported strikes, and then a dramatic drop in the most recent year for which there is data, 2017. Why the sudden decrease in reported strikes not seen for a full decade? Was there some effective new technology implemented at airports all over the country? A mass migration of birds and animals south? A strike by the FAA employees responsible for managing the data?

The answer that's immediately obvious as soon as you know it is that we're only looking at an extract that includes partial data for 2017. If we increase the level of granularity to month or week, we can see that the data only goes through roughly the middle of the year in 2017 (Figure 4.2).

To be exact, the latest recorded wildlife strike in our data set reportedly occurred on July 31, 2017, at 11:55:00 p.m. The earliest recorded wildlife strike in the extract occurred on January 1, 2000,

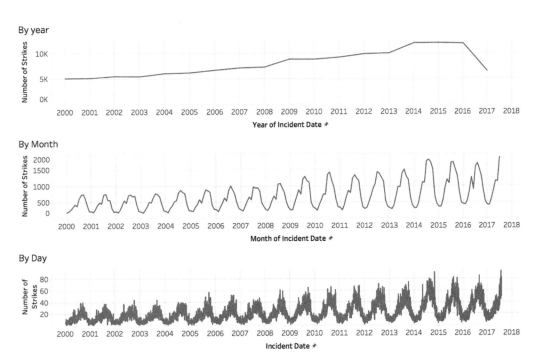

FIGURE 4.2 Visualizing reported collisions by various levels of data aggregation.

at 9:43:00 a.m. This is the range of our data in terms of reported collision dates, and brings us to an important tip to help us avoid falling into the common pitfall of mistaking mismatching levels of aggregation with actual trends in the data:

Explore the contours of your data to become acquainted with the minimum and maximum values of all measures in the data source, and their ranges.

If you'll permit me a brief tangent for a moment, I have to credit my friend Michael Mixon (on Twitter @mix_pix) for introducing me to the phrase "explore the contours of your data." He mentioned it in a discussion some years ago and it has stuck with me ever since, because it's perfect. It reminds me to make sure I spend a little bit of time upfront finding out the boundaries of the data I'm analyzing – the minimum and maximum values of each quantitative measure in the data set, for example – before coming to any conclusions about what the data says.

I imagine it's not unlike coming upon an uncharted island, like the Polynesians who first discovered and settled New Zealand around 700 years ago and became the Maori people. Or similar to the explorer James Cook who, in late 1769 through early 1770, was the first European to completely circumnavigate the pair of islands that make up the native home of the Maori (Figure 4.3).

What's interesting is that Cook actually wasn't the first European to find New Zealand. Over a century before him, in 1642, the Dutch navigator Abel Tasman came upon it in his ship the *Zeehaen*, but he didn't go fully around it or explore its shores nearly as thoroughly as Cook did. That's why Cook's expedition correctly identified the area between the north and south islands of New Zealand as a *strait* and therefore a navigable waterway, not a *bight* – merely a bend or curve in the coastline without passage through – as the Dutchman mistakenly thought it to be. And that's why that area between the north and south islands of New Zealand is called Cook Strait[3] instead of

---

[3] https://en.wikipedia.org/wiki/Cook_Strait.

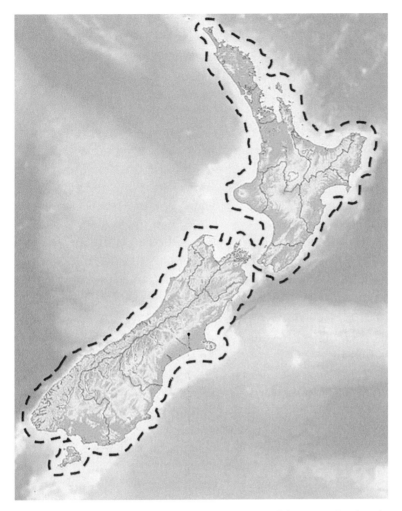

FIGURE 4.3   An imagined circumnavigation of the New Zealand island pair.

Source: https://en.wikipedia.org/wiki/Cook_Strait. Used under CC BY-SA 3.0.

Zeehaen's Bight, as Tasman originally named it. It's a great object lesson for us, because it shows how, when we fail to thoroughly explore the contours, we can arrive upon mistaken and erroneous conclusions about the terrain, in navigation just as in data.

Okay, thanks for humoring me with that brief digression – back to our wildlife strikes data set. Now it may seem silly that someone would assume a partial year was actually a full year, especially when the data so obviously drops off precipitously. Most people would figure that out right away, wouldn't they? You'd be surprised. Whenever I show this timeline to students in my data visualization classes and ask them what could explain the dramatic decline in reported strikes in 2017, they come up with a whole host of interesting theories like the ones I mentioned above, even when I'm careful to use the word "reported" in my question. It's very much related to the data-reality gap we talked about a couple of chapters ago; in this case we make the erroneous assumption that the data point for "2017" includes *all* of 2017.

There are times, though, when our particular angle of analysis makes it even less likely that we'll be aware that we're looking at partial data in one or more levels of our aggregated view. What if we wanted to explore seasonality of wildlife strikes – do strikes occur most often in winter months or summer months, for example? If we went about seeking an answer to this question without first exploring the contours of our data, we would start our analysis with a view of total reported strikes by month for the entire data set. Figure 4.4 shows what we'd create very quickly and easily with today's powerful analytics and visualization software.

One of our first observations would likely be that the month with the greatest number of reported wildlife strikes is July. The number of strikes is at its lowest in the winter months of December, January, and February, and then the count slowly increases through the spring, dipping slightly from May to June before surging to reach its peak in July. After this peak, the counts steadily decline month by month.

Well, what we already know from exploring our data's contours previously is that the records end on July 31, 2017, so there is *one extra month of data* included in the bars for January through July than for August through December. If we add yearly segments to the monthly bars – one segment for each year with data – and color only the 2017 segments red, we see that comparing each month in this way isn't strictly an apples-to-apples comparison (Figure 4.5):

Strikes by month, all years

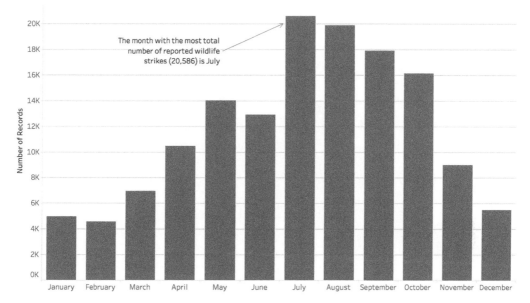

FIGURE 4.4   Wildlife strikes by month.

January, February, March, April, May, June, and July all include data from 18 different years, and the rest of the months only include data for 17 different years because 2017 is a partial year in our particular data set. If we filter out the 2017 data from the data set entirely, then we take off the red segments from the bars above, and each monthly bar includes data for the exact same number of years. Once we do so, we quickly notice that July isn't actually the month with the most number of reported wildlife strikes at all (Figure 4.6).

August, not July, is the month with the highest total number of strikes when we adjust the bounds of our data so that monthly comparisons are closer to an apples-to-apples comparison. We see a slight increase in reported strikes from July to August, and then the counts steadily drop after that, month by month, until the end of the year.

If we went away from a quick and cursory analysis thinking July is the peak month, we'd be just like Abel Tasman sailing away from the Cook Strait thinking surely the shoreline must be closed off to

Strikes by month, bars segmented by years

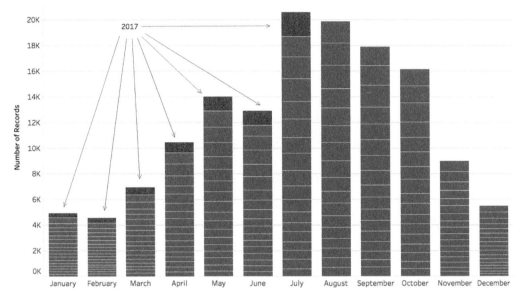
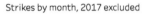

FIGURE 4.5   Wildlife strikes by month, with added yearly bar segments.

Strikes by month, 2017 excluded

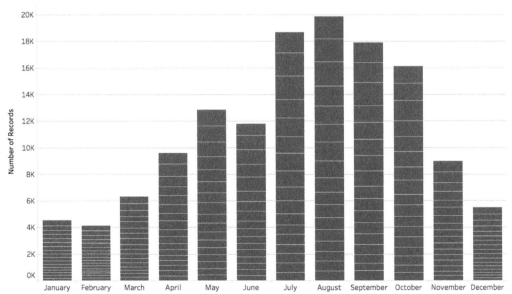

FIGURE 4.6   Wildlife strikes by month, with yearly segments, 2017 data excluded.

passage through. How many times have we been mistaken about a basic fact about our data because we simply overlooked the boundaries of the data set with which we are interacting?

Pitfall 3B: Missing Values

There's another issue that pops up quite often when aggregating data and comparing across categories. We've just seen that quirks related to the outer boundaries of our data can give us confusing results if we're not careful, but sometimes there can be idiosyncrasies in the interior regions of the data as well, away from the extreme values. To illustrate this pitfall, let's step cautiously into a rather haunted realm.

I became interested one particular day in visualizing the complete works of American author and poet Edgar Allan Poe. The day happened to be October 7, the anniversary of his mysterious death in Baltimore at the age of 40. As I sit down to write this chapter, I'm 40 years old as well, but I can still recall reading a number of his dark and chilling works back in middle school and high school. Who could forget works such as "The Raven," "The Tell-Tale Heart," and "The Cask of Amontillado"?

But I wondered just how prolific a writer he had been over the course of his life. I had no idea how many works in total he had written or published, at what age he started and stopped, and whether he had particular droughts of production during that time.

Luckily, I stumbled on a Wikipedia page of his entire bibliography containing tables of each of his known works organized by type of literature and sorted by the date each work was written.[4] There are about 150 works in all, with a few that are disputed. That's certainly more than I've read, and far more than I expected to find out that he had written; I had guessed a few dozen at most.

---

[4] https://en.wikipedia.org/wiki/Edgar_Allan_Poe_bibliography.

The tables on the Wikipedia page sometimes provide a complete date for a particular work, sometimes only and month and year is listed, and other times just the year. If we clean up these tables a little and create a timeline of the count of works written by Edgar Allan Poe by year, here's what we see (Figure 4.7).

We can see right away that he started writing in 1824, the year he would've turned 15, and he wrote up until and including the year of his death, 1849. It looks like his most productive year, at least in terms of the number of different works written, was 1845, when he wrote 13 pieces. Now, consider – in which year of his career did he produce the fewest number of works?

If you're like me, your eyes will immediately look for the lowest points on the timeline – namely, the points for 1824 and 1825 with a value of 1. In each of those two years, Poe wrote just one single work of literature. We'll give him a break, because he was just a teenager in those years. There we go, final answer: he wrote the fewest pieces of literature in 1824 and 1825.

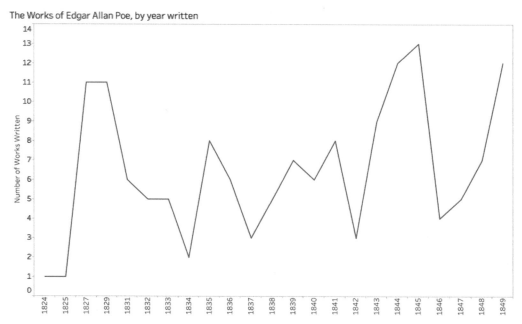

FIGURE 4.7   A timeline of the complete works of Edgar Allan Poe by year published.

Of course, by now you've come to expect that your first answer to questions I pose in this book is almost always wrong, and that's true in this case, as well. Those are not the years in which he wrote the fewest pieces of literature. If you find yourself in the bottom of that pitfall right now, don't feel bad; a number of your fellow readers are right down there with you, and so was I. The key, as always, is to look much more closely, just like Sherlock Holmes examining a crime scene.

The years march along the horizontal axis one after another in sequence, but if you examine the values, you'll notice that there are a few years missing in the series. There are no values on the x-axis for 1826, 1828, and 1830. In those years, Poe evidently published nothing. What's tricky, though, is that because the years are being treated as qualitative ordinal and not quantitative (this was the default of the software package I used for this chart, Tableau Desktop), it's difficult to notice that these years are missing from the timeline. Even the slopes around these years are skewed.

We might be tempted to switch from a discrete variable to a continuous one on the horizontal axis, but this actually makes matters worse, making it seem as if Poe wrote 6 works in 1826, 11 in 1828, and then about 8.5 in 1830 (Figure 4.8).

The x-axis may not skip any values in this iteration like it did in the first one, but the lines are still drawn from point to point and don't give a proper sense of a break in the values. His three nonproductive years are completely hidden from us in this view. If this is all we saw and all we showed to our audience, we'd be in the dark about his actual productivity pattern.

In order to clearly see the missing years – the years with zero works written – we'll need to switch back to discrete years on the horizontal axis (creating headers or "buckets" of years once again instead of a continuous axis as in the previous iteration), and tell the software to show missing values at the default location, zero. Doing so provides us with the much more accurate view shown in Figure 4.9.

The Works of Edgar Allan Poe, continuous years

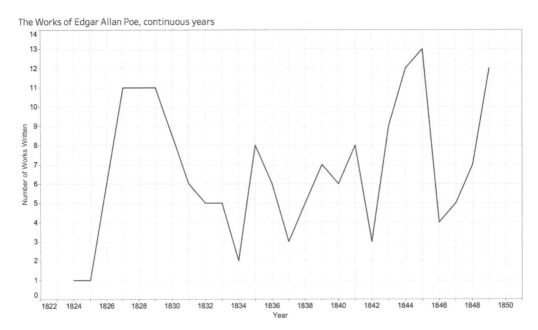

FIGURE 4.8   A timeline of Poe's works with years plotted continuously on the x-axis.

The Works of Edgar Allan Poe, showing missing years as zero output

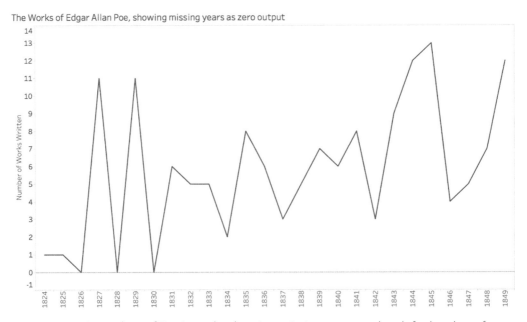

FIGURE 4.9   A timeline of Poe's works showing missing years at the default value of zero.

We could also elect to plot the data as a series of columns instead of as a continuous line, and we could create a box for each work to give a better sense of the heights of the columns without requiring the reader to refer to the y-axis, as seen in Figure 4.10.

Now I want to stress that I didn't go to any great lengths to doctor the first two misleading views with the intent to confuse you and write a book about it. Not at all, and that's not the point of this book. The two misleading views of Poe's works are how the software plotted my data by default, and that's exactly the problem to which I'm trying to alert you.

It's not a problem with this particular software, per se. It's a problem with how we decide to handle missing values. We'll approach this problem differently in different circumstances. If we were looking at election statistics or data from the summer games, for example, would we necessarily want the timeline to drop to zero every time we come across a year without data? No, because we know these events only happen every two or four years or so. In those cases, the default would probably work just fine.

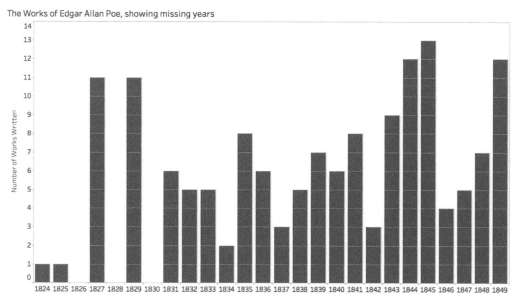

FIGURE 4.10   Poe's works depicted as columns, with missing years shown.

Missing values within our data set are dangerous lurkers waiting to trip us up, but there's another type of snag about which to be alert.

Pitfall 3C: Tripping on Totals

I have a special relationship with this next pitfall, because I actually fell into it while trying to warn people about it. You have to learn to laugh at yourself about this stuff. I was at the University of Southern California just this past year, conducting a training session for journalists specializing in health data. I mentioned to them that I was writing this very chapter of this very book, and that I'd be alerting them to various pitfalls during the course of my presentation and workshop.

When I conduct training sessions, I prefer, whenever possible, to work with data that's interesting and relevant to the audience. This is a tricky business because that means I'll be showing them data on a topic about which they're familiar, and at the same time I myself am not. It actually makes it fun, though, because I get to be the learner and ask them questions about the field while they get to learn from me about working with data.

At this particular workshop, since it was in my former home state of California, I elected to visualize infectious diseases – sorted by county, year, and sex – contracted by California residents from 2001 through 2015, with data provided by the Center for Infectious Diseases within the California Department of Public Health.[5] I made a very lame joke about how we'd be working with some really dirty data, and then we dived right in.

The first question we asked of the data was a simple one: how many total infectious diseases were reportedly contracted by California residents over this time period? By totaling the number of records in the data set, the answer we got was 15,002,836 (Figure 4.11).

---

[5] https://data.chhs.ca.gov/dataset/infectious-disease-cases-by-county-year-and-sex.

Reported Infectious Diseases, California Residents, 2001-2015

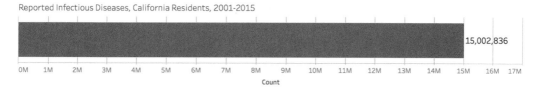

FIGURE 4.11 Reported infectious diseases.

But I have to admit, it was a total setup. I had looked at the data beforehand, and I knew there was something funky about the way the file was structured. Every county, year, and disease combination had three rows in the spreadsheet: one for male residents, one for female residents, and another for the total number of residents, so male plus female. Figure 4.12 is a snapshot of the first 10 entries in the data set.

What this means, then, is that a simple SUM function of the Count column will result in a total that accounts for each case twice. Each case of a male resident of California contracting a disease is counted twice, once in the row where Sex is equal to "Male" and another time in the row where Sex is equal to "Total." Same goes for female.

_id	Disease	County	Year	Sex	Count	Population	Rate	CI.lower	CI.upper	Unstable
1	Amebiasis	California	2001	Female	176	17339700	1.015	0.871	1.177	
2	Amebiasis	California	2001	Male	365	17173042	2.125	1.913	2.355	
3	Amebiasis	California	2001	Total	541	34512742	1.568	1.438	1.705	
4	Amebiasis	California	2002	Female	145	17554666	0.826	0.697	0.972	
5	Amebiasis	California	2002	Male	279	17383624	1.605	1.422	1.805	
6	Amebiasis	California	2002	Total	424	34938290	1.214	1.101	1.335	
7	Amebiasis	California	2003	Female	127	17782868	0.714	0.595	0.85	
8	Amebiasis	California	2003	Male	261	17606060	1.482	1.308	1.674	
9	Amebiasis	California	2003	Total	388	35388928	1.096	0.99	1.211	
10	Amebiasis	California	2004	Female	101	17968347	0.562	0.458	0.683	

Showing 1 to 10 of 166,557 entries

FIGURE 4.12 First 10 entries in the data set.

So I asked them next what else they would like to know about infectious diseases reported right here in California, and of course a budding data journalist in the audience raised a hand and, as if planted ahead of time, asked, "Are there more for male or female?"

I smiled a Grinch-like smile and proclaimed that I thought the question was a marvelous one, and I prompted them to look for the answer by adding Sex to the bar color encoding, as seen in Figure 4.13.

There was a moment of silence in the room as the confused students looked at the bar, and I, in what was probably a very unconvincing way, feigned shock at the result.

"What have we here? There is a value in the Sex attribute called 'Total' that accounts for 50% of the total reported diseases. That means we're double counting, doesn't it? There aren't 15 million reported infectious disease cases in California from 2001 to 2015, there are only half of that amount, around 7.5 million. Our first answer was off by factor of 2! I told you we'd fall into our share of pitfalls. This one is called 'Trespassing Totals,' because the presence of a 'Total' row in the data can cause all sorts of problems with aggregations."

My soapbox speech was over, the students considered themselves duly warned, and the instructor considered himself pretty darn smart. We went on with the analysis of this same data set.

Not too far down the road of data discovery, we began to explore infectious disease counts by county. Naturally, we created a map (Figure 4.14):

Reported Infectious Diseases, California Residents, 2001-2015

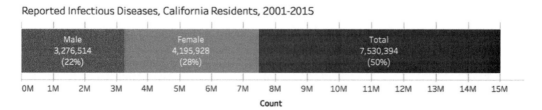

FIGURE 4.13   Reported infectious diseases.

Reported Infectious Diseases, California Residents, by County

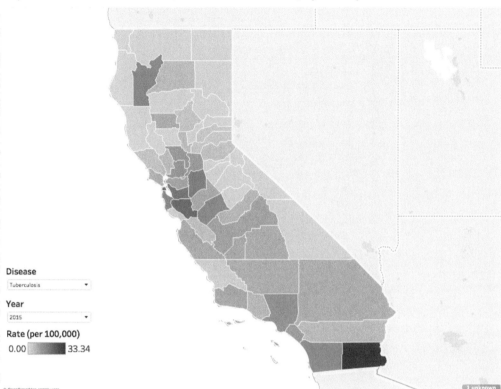

Disease

Tuberculosis ▾

Year

2015 ▾

Rate (per 100,000)

0.00 ▮▮▮ 33.34

© OpenStreetMap contributors

1 unknown

FIGURE 4.14 Choropleth map for tuberculosis infections, 2015.

We were moving right along, but then one of the trainees asked, "Hey, Ben, what does the '1 unknown' message in the bottom right corner of the map mean?"

I hadn't noticed it at first, so I clicked on it, and what I saw made me stop for a moment, and then I burst out laughing. There was a row for each disease and year combination for each county, but there was an additional row with the county "California" (Figure 4.15).

Why was that so funny? Well, New York state has a New York county, but California definitely doesn't have a California county. I can only imagine that the people who created and published the data set wanted to include a row for each disease and year combination that

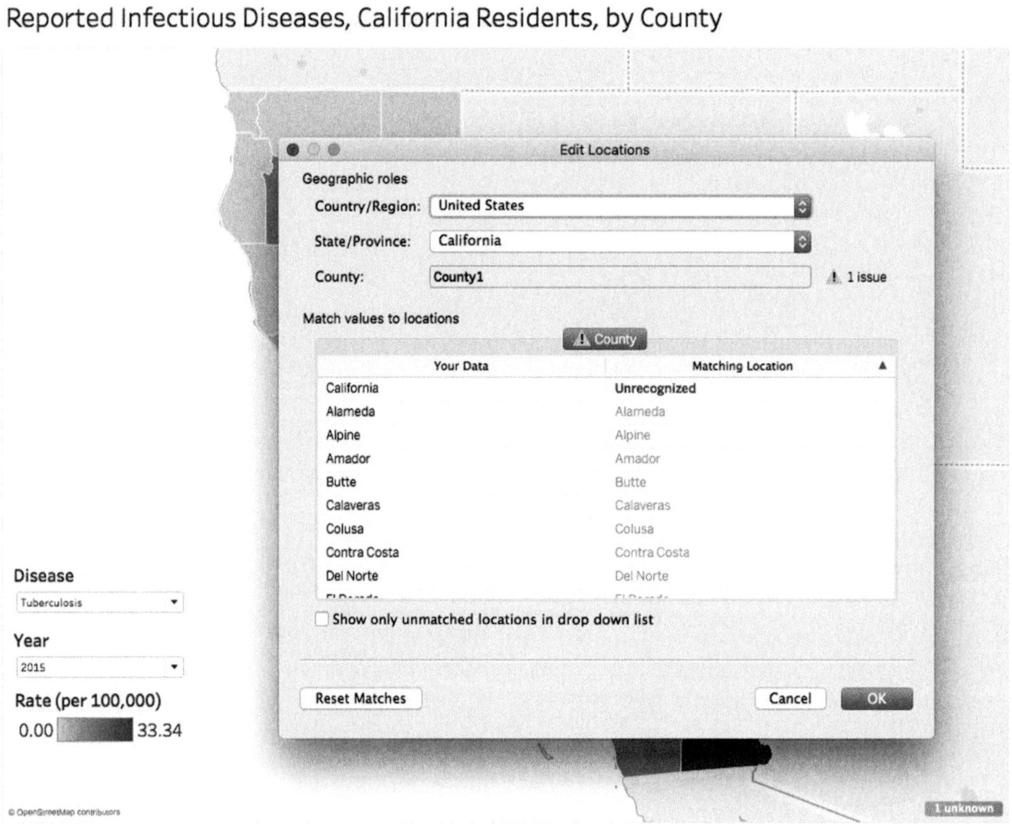

Reported Infectious Diseases, California Residents, by County

FIGURE 4.15   Geographic roles.

provided the reported cases for all of the counties added together, and they used the state name as a placeholder for "All counties."

This fact by itself isn't really very funny at all, I admit, but what it meant was the answer to our initial question of how many total infectious diseases had been reported – 15 million – wasn't off by a factor of 2, it was off by a factor of 4! The actual number isn't 7.5 million, it's 3.74 million. We were counting twice for each gender, and then twice again for each county because of pesky total rows.

The very pitfall I was trying to show them was one I had fallen into twice as deep as I thought I had. Data sure has a way of humbling us, doesn't it?

So we've seen how aggregating data can result in some categories being empty, or null, and how we can sometimes miss interesting findings when we rely on software defaults and don't look closely enough at the view. We've also seen how pesky total rows can be found within our data, and can make even the simplest answers wrong by an order of magnitude.

We need to be aware of these aspects of our data before we jump to conclusions about what the views and the results of our analysis are telling us. If we don't explore the contours of our data, as well as its interior, we're at risk of thinking some trends exist when they don't, and we're at risk of missing some key observations.

Aggregating data is a relatively simple mathematical operation (some would even call it trivial), and yet we've seen how even these basic steps can be tricky. Let's consider what happens when we do something slightly more involved, mathematically: working with ratios.

Pitfall 3D: Preposterous Percents

Let's switch topics to show another way in which our faulty math can lead us astray when we analyze data. Our next example deals with percents – very powerful, but often very tricky figures to work with. Each year the World Bank tabulates and publishes a data set that estimates the percent of each country's population that lives in an urban environment.[6] I love the World Bank's data team.

The timeline displayed on the World Bank site shows that the over-all worldwide figure for percent of urban population has increased from 33.6% in 1960 to 54.3% in 2016. This site also lets us download a data set of this proportion, which lets us drill down into the figures at a country and regional level.

With that data in hand, we can create a simple world map of the per-cent of each country that reportedly lived in an urban environment

---

[6] https://data.worldbank.org/indicator/SP.URB.TOTL.IN.ZS.

in 2016 (Figure 4.16). This map uses the viridis color palette[7] to show the countries of lower urban population (yellow and light green) and those with higher urban populations (blue to purple).

I don't know about you, but my eyes focus in on the yellow country shape in Africa, which is Eritrea. Did it really have an urban population of 0%, the value corresponding to bright yellow in the viridis color palette?

It turns out that it's not the only bright yellow country on the map, the other two are just too small to see – Kosovo and Saint Martin. Kosovo is a partially recognized state and Saint Martin is an overseas collectivity of France, but Eritrea is a member of the African Union and the United Nations. Its largest city, Asmara, has about 650,000 people living in it.

Year: 2016

Pct Urban Population

0.00%   100.00%

© OpenStreetMap contributors

FIGURE 4.16   Percent of urban population in 2016, all countries included.

[7] https://cran.r-project.org/web/packages/viridis/vignettes/intro-to-viridis.html.

It turns out that the World Bank data set that we just downloaded has a null (blank) value for these countries. Why the values for these three countries is null isn't fully clear, but regardless of the rationale, our map defaulted the null value for these two countries to 0%, which is misleading to the viewer of the map, as far as Eritrea is concerned (Figure 4.17).

We can exclude these three countries from the map, leaving an updated world map showing percent of urban population by country, with no nulls included (Figure 4.18).

Fair enough – our map is now less misleading, but what if we wanted to analyze percent of urban population at a *regional* level instead of at a country level? For example, what percent of North American residents lived in a city in 2016?

Lucky for us, the World Bank includes a region data field for each country, and the region North America includes the United States, Canada, and Bermuda (Mexico is included in the Latin America and Caribbean region). We can quickly list out the percent of urban population for each of these three countries, as shown in Figure 4.19.

But how do we determine the percent for the entire region from these three country-level figures? Clearly adding them up to get 263.80% would be silly and no one would ever sum percents that don't have a common denominator like that (I've done it more than once).

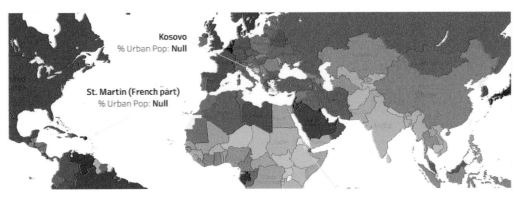

FIGURE 4.17   Percent of urban population in 2016, all countries included.

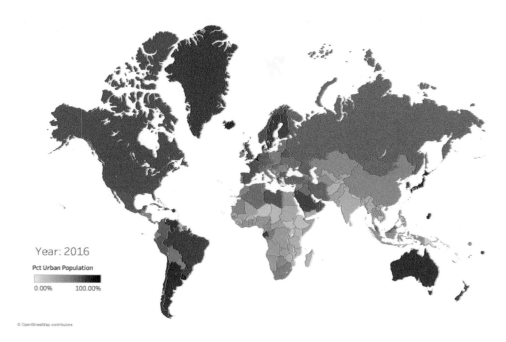

FIGURE 4.18   Percent of urban population in 2016, null values excluded.

Percent Urban Population, 2016

Region	Country Name	Pct Urban Population
North America	Bermuda	100.00%
	Canada	82.01%
	United States	81.79%

FIGURE 4.19   Table showing percent of urban population for countries in North America.

Clearly the answer is to average these values, right? So, a simple arithmetic average of the three countries in North America can be obtained by adding them up to get 263.80%, and then dividing that figure by 3 (one for each country). When we do that, we compute an average percent of urban population of 87.93% for the region (Figure 4.20).

Percent Urban Population, 2016

Region	Country Name	Pct Urban Population
North America	Bermuda	100.00%
	Canada	82.01%
	United States	81.79%
Average		**87.93%**

FIGURE 4.20 Computing the regional percent using the arithmetic average, or mean (wrong!).

Done and done! Right?

Wrong. We can't combine these percents in this way. It's a very common pitfall. Why can't we just average the percents? It's easy enough to do with modern spreadsheet and analytics software. If it's so easy to do with software, isn't it probably correct? Not even close. That's why I'm writing this book, remember?

The problem is related to the fact that each of the percents is a quotient of two numbers. The numerator for each quotient is the number of people who live in an urban environment in that particular country, and the denominator is the total population in that particular country.

So the denominators aren't the same at all (Figure 4.21).

When we ask about the urban population of North America, we're looking for the total number of people living in cities in North America divided by the total population of North America. But if

$$\frac{\text{Urban population of US}}{\text{Total population of US}}, \quad \frac{\text{Urban population of Canada}}{\text{Total population of Canada}}, \quad \frac{\text{Urban population of Bermuda}}{\text{Total population of Bermuda}}$$

FIGURE 4.21 Percent of urban population for each country shown as a quotient.

we remember back to fourth-grade math, when we add quotients together, we don't add the denominators, only the numerators (when the denominators are common). So in other words, we could only legitimately add the quotients together if each of the countries all had the exact same population. We don't even know the populations of each country, because those figures aren't included in the data set we downloaded.

So it seems we're at an impasse then, and unable to answer our question at the regional level. With just this data set, that's true, we can't. I think that part of the problem is that it *feels like we should be able to answer the question* at the regional level. Each country has a value, and each country is grouped into regions. It's simple aggregation, right? Yes, it's simple to do that math. And that's why pitfalls are so dangerous.

We could do that exact aggregation and answer the question at the regional level if we were analyzing values that aren't rates, ratios, or percentages, such as total population. That would be fine. There are no denominators to worry about matching with non-quotient values.

As it turns out, the total population data set is the missing key that can help us get where we want to go with our regional question with percent of urban population. And luckily the World Bank also publishes a separate data set with total population figures for each country over time.[8] Did I mention that I love the World Bank's data team?

If we download and blend or join the data set for country population, we can add the total population figures to the original table. Doing so shows us right away why we ran into trouble with our original arithmetic average approach – the populations of these three countries are drastically different (Figure 4.22).

Using this table, it would be fairly straightforward to determine the denominator for our regional quotient – the total population of

---

[8] https://data.worldbank.org/indicator/SP.POP.TOTL.

Percent Urban Population, 2016

Region	Country Name	Pct Urban Population	Total population
North America	Bermuda	100.00%	65,376
	Canada	82.01%	36,264,604
	United States	81.79%	323,127,513

FIGURE 4.22 Table with both percent of urban population and total population.

North America (as defined by the World Bank). We could just add the three numbers in the final column to get 359,457,493.

So now all we need is the total urban population of each country, which we can estimate by multiplying the percent of urban population by the total population for each country. Once we have that, we can easily calculate the regional quotient by dividing these two numbers together to get 81.81% (Figure 4.23).

Looking at this table, we can see that the regional percent of urban population is very close to the value for the United States. It's only two hundredths of a percent higher than the U.S. value,

Percent Urban Population, 2016

Region	Country Name	Calc Urban Pop Pct (for aggregation)	Total population	Calculated Urban Pop
North America	Bermuda	100.00%	65,376	65,376
	Canada	82.01%	36,264,604	29,739,151
	United States	81.79%	323,127,513	264,279,530
Grand Total		**81.81%**	**359,457,493**	**294,084,057**

FIGURE 4.23 Table showing percent of urban population, total population, and estimated urban population.

to be precise. And the reason for this is obvious now: the United States dominates the population in the region, with almost 90% of the inhabitants living there. Bermuda, which has 100% of its residents living in a city, only accounts for less than 0.02% of the total population of the region. So to give them equal weighting when determining the regional average wouldn't be accurate at all.

Another way to look at this is to place each of the three countries on a scatterplot of urban population versus percent of urban population, size the circles by population, and add both regional percentages – the correct one and the incorrect one (Figure 4.24).

It was convenient to show this pitfall and how to avoid it step by step for North America because there are only three countries listed in the region, so the full regional table is easy to show. A similar analysis, however, could be done for each of the regions

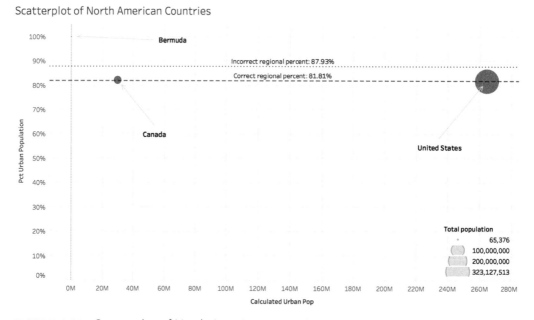

FIGURE 4.24   Scatterplot of North American countries.

in the World Bank data set. If we did so, we could create the slopegraph seen in Figure 4.25, which shows how the incorrect urban percents compare with the correct urban percents for each region. Notice how wrong we would've been for the Latin America and Caribbean region, which jumps up from 65% to over 80% urban when we take into account population instead of just averaging the values for each country.

This seems like a simple error, and once you see it you can't imagine ever falling into this pitfall. But it's very easy to overlook the signs and fall headfirst into it. You get that face-palm feeling every time you find yourself down there. After a while, you spot it quite quickly. Be very careful when aggregating rates, ratios, percents, and proportions. It's tricky business.

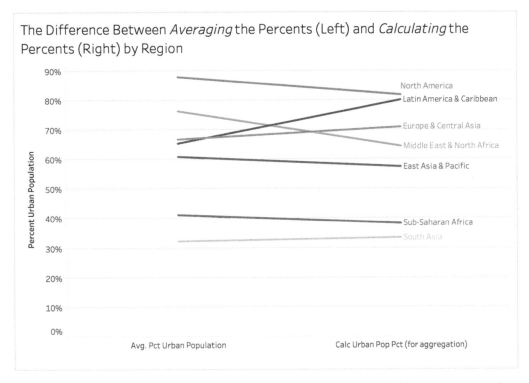

FIGURE 4.25 Slopegraph showing difference between incorrect (left) and correct (right) regional percents.

Pitfall 3E: Unmatching Units

The next aspect of this common pitfall has to do with the way we measure things. When we perform mathematical operations on different quantities in our data, we need to make sure we're aware of the units of measure involved. If we don't take care, we might not be dealing with an apples-to-apples scenario, and we might end up with highly erroneous results from our calculations.

I already mentioned the infamous example of the Mars Climate Orbiter (Figure 4.26) at the beginning this chapter. What happened was that the orbiter traveled far too close to the surface of Mars and likely incinerated as a result. The cause for this faulty trajectory was

FIGURE 4.26 Artist's rendering of the Mars Climate Orbiter.
Source: https://en.wikipedia.org/wiki/Mars_Climate_Orbiter#/media/File:Mars_Climate_Orbiter_2.jpg. Public domain.

that a Lockheed Martin software system on earth output thruster firing impulse results in pound-force seconds (lbf-s), while a second system created by NASA expected those results in Newton-seconds (N-s) based on the specification for each system. One pound-force is equal to 4.45 Newtons, so the calculation resulted in a lot less thrust than the orbiter actually needed to stay at a safe altitude. The total cost for the mission was $327.4 million, and perhaps a bigger loss was the delay in acquiring valuable information about the surface and atmosphere of our neighbor in the solar system.

I recall that while going through engineering school at the University of California at Los Angeles in the late 1990s, units of measure were a big deal. As students, we would routinely be required to convert from the International System of Units (SI, abbreviated from the French Système international d'unités) to English Engineering units and vice versa on assignments, lab experiments, and exams. It would've been a rookie mistake to forget to convert units. My classmates and I made such rookie mistakes all the time.

It's really easy to sit back and whine about this situation. After all, only three countries in the world at present don't use the metric system as the national system of units: Liberia, Myanmar, and the United States. Try to imagine, though, if you lived in antiquity, when traveling to another neighboring town meant encountering a totally unique system of measuring length, mass, and time, often based on a local feudal lord's thumb size or foot length or something like that.

We have the French Revolution to thank for the pressure to adopt a common set of units of measure. And we're close. The cost for the United States to switch every road sign, every law, every regulatory requirement, every package label would be massive and those costs would be incurred over years or even decades. But how much more could be saved in reduced errors, streamlined cross-border trade, and international communications over the long run? You can tell which side I'm on, not because I'm a globalist (I am), but because I'm in favor of making data pitfalls less menacing. Hence, this book.

For those of my dear readers who aren't engineers or scientists, you're probably sitting there thinking to yourself, "Phew, I sure am glad I don't have to worry about this problem! After all, I don't design Mars Orbiters or Rovers or anything like that."

First, let's all acknowledge how cool it would be to design Mars Orbiters and Rovers and literally everything like that.

Second, not so fast. You have to consider units of measure, too. You know it's true. Ever put a tablespoon of salt into a dish instead of the teaspoon the recipe calls for? Me too. Yuck.

Here are ten different ways I've fallen to the very bottom of this nasty pitfall in a variety of contexts, including business contexts:

- Calculating cost or revenue with different currencies: U.S. dollars versus euros versus yen
- Calculating inventory with different units of measure: "eaches" (individual units) versus boxes of 10, or palettes of 10 packages of 10 boxes
- Comparing temperatures: Celsius versus Fahrenheit (versus Kelvin)
- Doing math with literally any quantity, where suffixes like K (thousands), M (millions), and B (billions) are used
- Working with location data when latitude and longitude are expressed in degrees minutes seconds (DMS) versus decimal degrees (dd)
- Working with 2-D spatial location using cartesian (x,y) versus polar (r,θ) coordinates
- Working with angles in degrees versus radians
- Counting or doing math with values in hexadecimal, decimal, or binary
- Determining shipping dates when working with calendar days versus business days

Some of these items on the list above are quite tricky and we encounter them on a fairly regular basis. Take the last one, for example – shipping duration. When, exactly, will my package arrive, taking into account weekends and holidays? And is it U.S. holidays, or do I need to consider Canadian or UK holidays, too? Technically, the base unit of measure is one day regardless, but we're measuring time in groups of certain *types* of days. It may seem like a technicality, but it could mean the difference between getting that critical package on time and having to go on our trip without it.

The best way to fall into this pitfall is to dive into a data set without taking time to consult the metadata tables. Metadata is our best friend when it comes to understand what, exactly, we're dealing with, and why it's critical to rigorously document the data sets we create. A data field might be entitled "shipping time," but what is the operational definition of this field? Another data field might be entitled "quantity," but is that measured in units, boxes, or something else? Yet another data field is called "price," but what is the currency?

We always need to consult the metadata. If there is no metadata, we need to demand it. Every time I've worked with a data set that has been rigorously documented – with each field described in detail so as to answer my unit of measure questions, among others – I've appreciated the time spent on defining every field.

One detail to watch out for is that sometimes a data set will have a field that includes records with different units – a mixed data field. Often, in those cases, there's a second accompanying column, or data field, that specifies the unit of measure for each field. Those are particularly complex cases where we might need to write IF/THEN calculations based on the unit of measure (often "UoM") field in order to convert all values into common units prior to performing simple aggregation calculations like Sum and Average.

In this chapter I attempted to give a sense of the kinds of mathematical errors that I've come across, but there are a great many others that I didn't mention. Every data set will challenge us in some way mathematically, and the impact could amount to orders of magnitude errors.

We're almost lucky when the erroneous result is ridiculously large (a population that's 2,000% urban?) because it becomes immediately clear that we've fallen into this pitfall. When the magnitude of the error is much smaller, though, we could be in big trouble, and we won't know it until it's too late, and all that expensive equipment is plummeting to its molten demise 225 million kilometers away.

But wait, how many miles would that be?

Chapter Five

Pitfall 4: Statistical Slipups

"Facts are stubborn things, but statistics are pliable."
—Mark Twain

How We Compare Data

In spite of the incredible utility and value of the field of statistics, its name has become somewhat of a byword in our time. Common search phrases that start with "statistics are" include:

- "statistics are bad"
- "statistics are lies"
- "statistics are useless"
- "statistics are not facts"
- "statistics are made up"
- "statistics are for losers"

What gives? Why such disgust for a field that, according to the Merriam-Webster dictionary, is simply "a branch of mathematics dealing with the collection, analysis, interpretation, and presentation of masses of numerical data."[1] Why is the field of statistics seen in such a negative light by so many?

I believe that the backlash against statistics is due to four primary reasons. The first, and easiest for most people to relate to, is that even the most basic concepts of descriptive and inferential statistics can be difficult to grasp and even harder to explain. Many a befuddled college freshman struggles to get a passing grade in Stats 101 each year. But even many professional scientists struggle to articulate what, exactly, a p-value is.[2]

The second cause for vitriol is that even well-intentioned experts misapply the tools and techniques of statistics far too often, myself included. Statistical pitfalls are numerous and tough to avoid. When we can't trust the experts to get it right, there's a temptation to throw the baby out with the bathwater.

The third reason behind all the hate is that those with an agenda can easily craft statistics to lie when they communicate with us. Even those in Mark Twain's day realized this, as this chapter's epigraph shows. There are quite popular how-to books written on the topic of lying with statistics for the would-be deceiver.[3]

And finally, the fourth cause is that often statistics can be perceived as cold and detached, and they can fail to communicate the human element of an issue. No one wants to wind up "being a statistic," a phrase equated with being the victim of an unfortunate circumstance and then being forever shrouded in anonymity via aggregation into a single, nameless, and faceless number. Whoa, talk about a negative connotation!

---

[1] https://www.merriam-webster.com/dictionary/statistics.
[2] http://fivethirtyeight.com/features/not-even-scientists-can-easily-explain-p-values/.
[3] https://www.amazon.com/How-Lie-Statistics-Darrell-Huff/dp/0393310728.

But in spite of these popular condemnations, the field of statistics provides vital tools in the toolkit of every data worker. In some ways, if you reconsider the definition cited above, *everything we do* when we work with data is actually just statistics, no matter what sexier name we might want to give it. Data analysis, analytics, data science – they're all just subsets of statistics, if we interpret the definition literally.

So how can we rescue the perception of the field of statistics from purgatory? How can we restore it to its rightful position as the "OG" data-working discipline? It starts with understanding the pitfalls that give it a bad name.

Pitfall 4A: Descriptive Debacles

The simplest and most basic branch of statistics is descriptive statistics – boiling a data set down to individual figures that describe or summarize the data set itself – nothing more, nothing less. Consider how often you come across figures similar to the following, for example:

- The median income of all employees in a company
- The range of SAT scores in a class
- The variance of returns in a portfolio of stocks
- The average height of players on a team

This branch of statistics is distinct from inferential statistics, where we seek to infer properties about an underlying (and usually much larger) population from which a sample was drawn. We'll get to that later.

But are there really pitfalls involved with something as simple as describing a data set using summary statistics? You bet there are. Anyone who works with data falls into these pitfalls all the time. We've already seen how we can screw up something as basic as aggregating data where the mathematical operation is addition. How much easier, then, is it to stumble when we apply even slightly more involved calculations like average and standard deviation? Where to start. . .

In the toolbox of descriptive statistics, measures of central tendency are the hammer – one of the most useful tools of all – but often used rather clumsily. Much has been written about mean, median, and mode, and I don't intend to approach the subject as a textbook would. Most of us know the formulas by now – mean is the sum of all values added together and then divided by the total number of values (also called the "arithmetic average," or just the "average"), median is the value above which you will find half of the records and below which you will find the other half, and mode is simply the value that appears most frequently in a particular data set.

It's not in calculating these statistics that the most common errors occur. The formulas are fairly straightforward, and scores of software packages compute them reliably. The real difficulty with these measures of central tendency is that when we use them, our audience interprets them as *normal* or *typical* values to which most of the records in the data set must surely be similar. Depending on the distribution of the data, that can be an accurate impression, or a wildly inaccurate one. Consider an example from the world of sports.

Let's talk football. Okay, to be more specific, let's talk American football.

On average, a male player in the professional American football league in the United States is 25 years old, stands about 6'2" tall, weighs 244.7 pounds, makes $1.5 million dollars per year, wears the jersey number 51, and has 13 characters in his full name (including spaces, hyphens, etc.).

Those statements are mathematical facts, at least if we analyze the 2,874 active players on the 2018 preseason team rosters of the 32 teams in the North American professional American football league (the salary figure is based on the 2017 "cap hit" of 1,993 active players, since salary data for the 2018 season wasn't yet available when I wrote this).

And now that I've told you all that, you have in your mind an impression of what "typical" means in that particular sport and league.

If that information were all that I gave you, you'd probably think a player identified at random would have attributes fairly close to those provided averages, plus or minus some small amount of variation – within, say 10% or 20%.

You'd probably imagine a 50% deviation from the stated average to be highly unlikely (a 9'3" tall player?). You'd certainly have a hard time imagining any of their traits being in a completely different ballpark (pun intended) from the average values, right? Two or three times larger? Ten times larger than the average value? That seems pretty far-fetched.

And you'd be more or less right for about four of the six traits, for which the player with the maximum value doesn't even double the average. You'd be pretty close for a fifth trait, for which the player with the maximum value is about 2.25 times the average.

For another of the six traits, though, there's a chance that you'd be *drastically* wrong. One of the six traits possesses a different kind of variation altogether, and the player with the maximum value is *16 times greater than average*. We'll see in a moment which of the six traits has a variation like that. Perhaps you can already guess which one it is.

Let's analyze further. If I show you the distributions for each of these six attributes – histograms showing how many players fall into certain "bins" or groups of values on the spectrum from the minimum value on the left (not necessarily zero) to the maximum value on the right for each attribute, can you guess which histogram goes with which attribute? I'll remove all the axes and labels to make it more of a challenge (Figure 5.1).

Really test yourself. Examine the shape of each histogram and think about what it would mean if each attribute took on each of the respective shapes. For those of you who are less familiar with American football, this may be a tougher exercise than for those who know it well, but try anyway.

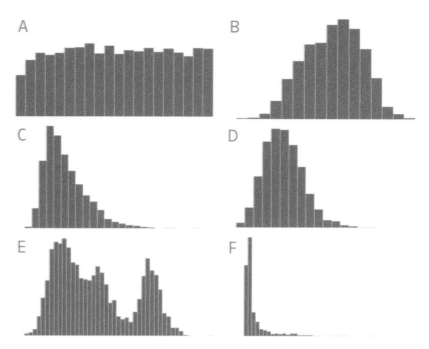

FIGURE 5.1   Guess which distribution shows age, weight, salary, height, jersey number, and name length of NFL players.

Let's pretend we're back in school. Stressful, I know.

I'll write the letter label of each chart and the variable name in alphabetical order in two columns, and you draw a line between the two based on your best guess as to the match (Figure 5.2).

Okay, let's try together. Take distribution A – it's a fairly uniform distribution, right? Could that distribution correspond to player age? If so, we'd expect a slightly lower likelihood of a player selected at random being at the lowest end of the age distribution (the first bar is a bit lower than the others), but after that it would be about equally likely that they have any age in the set of all ages.

But look at the far-right edge of this distribution – it ends rather suddenly, doesn't it? There's no tail at all to this first distribution. Could it be that players above a certain "cut-off" age suddenly disappear from the league altogether? This would only seem likely if

A   Age

B   Height

C   Name Length

D   Salary (Cap Hit)

E   Uniform Number

F   Weight

FIGURE 5.2   Match the histogram letter with the player variable type.

there were some rule preventing players from playing beyond a certain age, but we know that's not the case. There's no "forced retirement" at, say, age 40. Which of the six traits has a cut-off rule that limits the upper value in this way?

Okay, now let's jump down to distribution E. This one has a rather odd three-humped shape, doesn't it? It's called a multimodal distribution because the histogram has two or more distinct peaks. Which of the six traits seems like it could have three different subgroups within the overall set of player values? Could it be salary? Is there one group of players that make a lesser amount, others that are paid according to a slightly higher bar, and a final group that are paid even more still? It would seem that only a strange law of economics would produce such a distribution for salary, so that's not a likely match, is it? To figure out which of the six attributes goes along with distribution E, we'd need to think about which would have exactly three distinct "types" of players around which they tend to cluster in subgroups.

Okay, enough pontificating. Figure 5.3 is the answer key to our little stats quiz.

How did you do? How many of the six distributions did you get correct? Let's look at them one by one and consider more closely

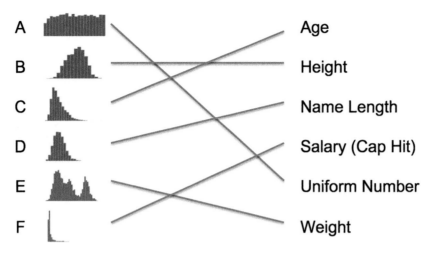

FIGURE 5.3   The distribution matching game answer key.

what the shape of the distribution means for the population of players, and how that relates to the notion we had developed in our minds about what a typical player looks like when we were just given the averages.

A. Uniform Distribution: Jersey Number

In a perfectly uniform distribution, a value chosen at random from the data set is equally likely to fall into any of the bins into which we group the data – like rolling a single six-sided die that's perfect weighted. Of course, empirical data sets from our world virtually never follow a distribution perfectly. But we can see from Figure 5.4 that if we group player jersey numbers into bins of 5 (players with jersey numbers 0–4 go into the first bin, those with jersey numbers 5–9 go into the second bin, 10 through 14 go into bin 3, and so on), each bin, with the exception of the first, accounts for about 5% of all of the players.

Why the drop-off after the last bar? It's simple: there's an official rule that all numbers on NFL jerseys have to be between 1 and 99.[4] This is why we see the series come to an abrupt

_____

[4] https://operations.nfl.com/the-rules/2018-nfl-rulebook/#article-2.-players-numbered-by-position.

Jersey Number

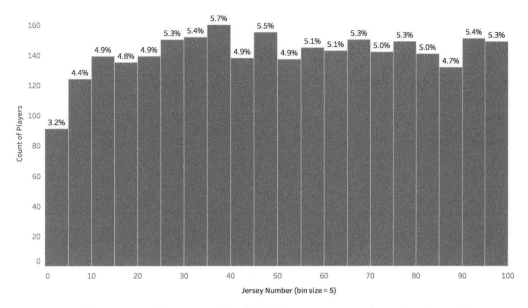

FIGURE 5.4 Histogram of American Football player jersey numbers, bin size = 5.

end after the last bar, which includes players who have jersey number 95 through 99. There are no players with a jersey number equal to 100.

So what does this distribution imply about our interpretation of the earlier statement that, on average, a player "wears the jersey number 51"? Well, first of all, we wouldn't be astronomically far off if we guessed that a player selected at random had jersey number 51. At most we'd be 50 steps away from the actual value, and there's a reason why the deviation from the actual value can't be any larger than that – namely, the jersey rule (provided the rule doesn't change).

Think of it this way: if the distribution for jersey number had a maximum value that was 16 times greater than the average, then there would be a player out on the field somewhere with the jersey number 816. I've watched a lot of football – too much – and that would definitely catch my eye.

What's even more interesting, though, is that only 27 of the 2,874 players on the 2018 active roster during the preseason were listed as having a jersey number of *exactly* 51, meaning we'd have less than a 1% chance of guessing it right if we went with the average for any particular player. Appropriately, only a player who plays the position "center" (the player in the middle of the offensive line who hikes the ball to the quarterback) is allowed to have this number, according to the official rules.

And other than avoiding the numbers 0 (only one player was listed on team rosters with a jersey number of 0 during the preseason months, likely erroneously) and 1 (only 16 active players were listed as having that number during the 2018 preseason), we'd have about a 1% chance of getting it right no matter which number we went with.

The jersey number with the highest frequency of occurrence in the entire league roster in 2018 is number 38 (coincidentally, 38 players were listed with jersey number 38 at the time I scraped the data

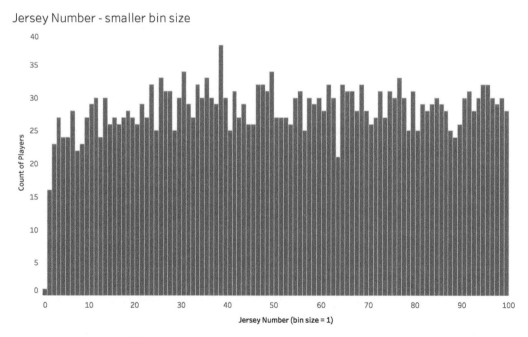

Jersey Number - smaller bin size

FIGURE 5.5 Smaller bin size.

from the web), and even then we'd still just have a 1.347% chance of getting it right. Figure 5.5 is the histogram modified to decrease the bin size to 1.

The bottom line is that when we have a uniform distribution, it's helpful to know the minimum and maximum values (and therefore the range, or the difference between these two numbers). The mean and median are both located in the center of the range and thus don't really provide any additional information for us, so long as we're aware that the distribution is uniform.

But is jersey number 51 a "typical" jersey number for an NFL player to wear? It's certainly within the range of what's possible, and of course we wouldn't say that it's atypical, like we would with jersey number 1. But "typical" doesn't really seem to capture it, either, does it? There aren't that many centers on each team, after all.

Let's move on to the next distribution.

B. Normal Distribution: Player Height

The heights of players in the NFL very much resembles a Gaussian, or normal, distribution. The normal curve is the most famous type of distribution, the basis of many statistical comparisons, a super-powerful tool, and also a source of blunders of epic proportions (Figure 5.6).

The average height of all of the players on the preseason rosters is 73.7 inches, or just under 6'2". The standard deviation of the distribution is 3.2 inches. What does that mean?

The standard deviation is often used to describe how much a particular distribution varies. So far in this chapter, we've been dividing the maximum value by the average to talk about how much each distribution varies (recall that one mystery distribution has a maximum that's 16 times greater than the average). That's a less effective way to talk about variation, though, because it depends highly on the magnitude of the amounts, and is only really meaningful to talk about distance from the average to the maximum value, not from the average to the minimum value.

Player Height

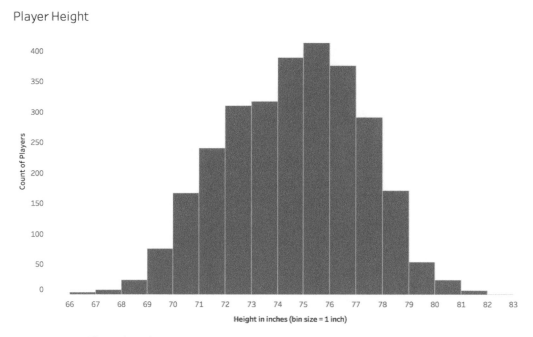

FIGURE 5.6   Player height.

Standard deviation (SD for short, sometimes indicated by the Greek letter σ) is calculated by taking the square root of the variance, which in turn is the expected value of the squared deviation from the mean. In the case of a normal, or Gaussian, distribution, the mean (μ) and the standard deviation (σ) together fully define the curve, as shown in Figure 5.7.

Sometimes people refer to the "68–95–99.7 Rule" when working with the Gaussian distribution, which tells us that about 68% of the values in a normally distributed data set can be found within plus or minus one standard deviation from the mean (34.1% + 34.1% to be exact), 95% can be found within two standard deviations from the mean (13.6% + 34.1% + 34.1% + 13.6%), and 99.7% can be found within three standard deviations from the mean (2.1% + the previous + 2.1%). It's a nice, perfectly symmetrical bell-shaped curve.

Where did this curve come from, and for what is it used? Before we go further in our discussion about football player attributes, let's take a brief aside into the history of statistics.

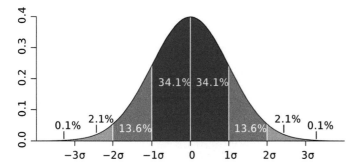

FIGURE 5.7   The standard normal distribution.
Source: https://en.wikipedia.org/wiki/Standard_deviation#/media/File:Standard_devia-tion_diagram.svg. Used under CC BY 2.5.

Gamblers in the eighteenth century used to employ statisticians to compute odds by hand in very time-consuming calculations. One such statistician, Abraham De Moivre, discovered that the odds of getting a certain number of heads or tails when flipping a coin multiple times approximated a bell-shaped curve more and more closely as the total number of coin flips increased. Galileo later discovered that the errors in astronomical measurements approximately fit a similar curve, leading to several hypotheses about the equation for the shape of this curve. At around the same time, mathematicians Robert Adrain and Carl Friedrich Gauss independently developed the equation for this curve in 1808 and 1809, respectively. The Belgian Adolphe Quetelet, developer of the body mass index (BMI), later applied the normal curve to social sciences and natural variables like human height, weight, and strength, just as we are analyzing here.

Starting in the late 1990s and thanks to former General Electric CEO Jack Welch, the "Six Sigma" movement introduced the concept of the normal curve and the standard deviation statistic to many business people who had never taken a single intro to stats class in college. The movement also reintroduced it to many others who had taken the dreaded freshman year course but had forgotten all about it.

The name for the movement had a "six" in front of it because a normal distribution in which the distance between the mean and both the upper and lower specification limits (what defines a "good" part in terms of quality control) is six times the standard deviation, or 6σ, will produce "good" parts 99.99966% of the time. That's a pretty good outcome for a manufacturing process that won't result in very much scrap or parts rejected due to out-of-specification measurements; 3.4 parts per million will be thrown away when you account for a 1.5σ "drift" in the process over time.

Enthusiasts of the movement eagerly applied the same way of measuring and improving processes to transactional processes as well as manufacturing ones, whether or not these processes exhibited stable outcomes that approximated the normal curve. More on that in a moment.

Another brief aside – I was a happy participant in the Six Sigma movement, earning the title "Master Black Belt" at my medical device employer and training eager "Green Belts" and "Black Belts" around the country in the ways of DMAIC, an acronym that described the 5 phases of a Six Sigma project: Define, Measure, Analyze, Improve, and Control. This movement was how I transitioned from an engineering career into a continuous improvement one.

I was super-proud about it all until my dad found out and asked me what the heck I was doing with the education he paid for. He was a pretty cool guy, and I think he was just trying to bust my chops, but there definitely was something almost hokey and/or cultish about the whole thing.

What can't be denied, though, is that people in historically non-statistically oriented departments like billing, customer service, and human resources started using – and undoubtedly misusing – statistics like the average and the standard deviation en masse. They were also comparing data sets using statistical hypothesis tests like the t-test, ANOVA, and the chi-squared test. It was a huge movement, and in some ways I feel that the more recent "big data" era (I hate that term) has left these important (if tricky for the layperson), hypothesis tests behind somewhat.

To return to our discussion of the football player heights, the fact that the distribution of heights closely approximates a normal

$$\frac{82 - \mu}{\sigma} = \frac{82 - 73.7}{3.2} = 2.6$$

FIGURE 5.8   Calculating the distance in standard deviations from the mean to the maximum value.

distribution means that the likelihood of finding a particular value in the set decreases rapidly the farther away you move from the mean. The tallest player in the data set, Nate Wozniak, was listed on the roster at 82 inches tall, or 6′10″, which is 2.6 times the standard deviation greater than the average value (Figure 5.8).

The value 2.6 is called the Z score, and we can look up the odds of being at least that far away from the mean using a Z score table for the normal distribution.[5] In the case of a group with average 73.7 inches and standard deviation 3.2 inches, the odds of being at least 82 inches tall is a little less than half a percent, or 0.47% to be exact. So about 1 in 215 players are expected to be as tall as Wozniak or taller.

A notable property of the normal curve, though, is that it never fully drops to 0. There's always some finite probability of being a certain distance away from the mean, no matter how far away you go. This probability gets vanishingly small as you get above, say, 10σ. A football player who is 6σ taller than the average would be almost 93 inches tall, or 7′9″, and the odds of finding a player with at least that height would be less than 1 in 1 billion.

C. Lognormal Distribution: Player Age

The truth, though, is that if you look at all six of our distributions, only one of them closely resembles the normal curve. The others depart from the Gaussian quite noticeably.

Take player age, for example. This distribution is said to be "right-skewed." Another way of describing it is that it displays "positive skewness" (Figure 5.9).

---

[5] http://www.z-table.com/.

Player Age

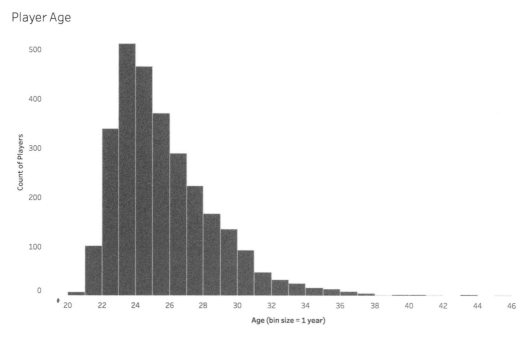

FIGURE 5.9   Player age.

The tail of players with ages higher than the mode, or the peak defined by the most common age group of 23 years old, is quite a bit longer than the tail of players with ages lower than the mode.

But wait a minute. You'll recall that we said at the beginning that the average player has an age of 25 years old, not 23 years old. The average is 25.22, to be exact. So why would the average be different than the peak of the histogram? If average is supposed to indicate "typical," why wouldn't it be equal to the age group that has the most total number of players in it?

The reason is that thinking that average always indicates "typical" is a statistical pitfall that we fall into over and over and over. This distribution, like many distributions, isn't symmetrical. Since there are more players to the right of the peak than to the left of it, these older players "pull" the mean to the right, away from the peak. You'll recall that the mean, or arithmetic average, is just the total sum of values, in this case ages, divided by the total count of items, in this case players.

The median age, the age at which half of the players are older and half are younger, is 25. When a distribution is skewed, either to the right or to the left, the median will be found between the mode (the peak) and the mean, or average. Which is "typical"? You tell me. They all make a claim. Their claims all fall short.

So why are there more older players than younger players, relatively speaking? It's an interesting question. Technically, there are no minimum or maximum age limits in the North American professional football league. But there is a rule that states that players must be out of high school for at least 3 years before playing professionally. So practically speaking, the youngest a player can be is 20 or in some rare cases 19 years old. This is a matter of some controversy, but we'll leave that alone for now; we're not interested in labor discrimination here as much as we are in the impact on the distribution.

On the other side of the coin, a player can continue playing for as long as they are capable of doing so. And some seem to have an uncanny ability to do so, especially kickers and punters like Adam Vinatieri (45 years old and the oldest player at the time of roster scraping) and Sebastian Janikowski, among others. I don't mean to make light of the risks that all football players take when stepping out onto the field, but let's be honest – players who play these positions are involved in relatively few plays from scrimmage, and don't often get hit very hard. Exceptions abound, of course.

As an aside, this distribution is similar to the shape of a survival function, which is often used in engineering to indicate the time it takes particular objects – it could be a patient or a device – to fail. If you think of the end of a football player's professional career as the point of "failure," then each player plays as long as they can until they can't play anymore, for one reason or another.

Instead of plotting the age of players at any given point of time, we'd exactly get a survival function if we plotted the length of time that each player played, from time = 0 when they started playing to time = x when they exit the league, in years, days, or whatever unit of time we'd like to use.

D. Normal Distribution (with Outlier): Number of Characters in Full Name

You may look at this fourth distribution – the number of characters in each player's name – and say, hey, this one looks like a normal curve, too! I agree, it does, but it has one interesting attribute that's hard to notice. Sure, it's also slightly right-skewed, but even more interestingly, it has an outlier value to the right that you can barely see (Figure 5.10).

The most common player name length is 12 characters, just slightly more than the number of players with 13 characters in their name. But there's a player with 29 total characters (including spaces and hyphens) in his name, and that's Christian Scotland-Williamson. The length of his name is almost 7 standard deviations higher than the mean. If there was a player whose height was that far away from the average height, he'd be over 7'8" tall. That wouldn't just be astronomically tall for a football player, that would be taller

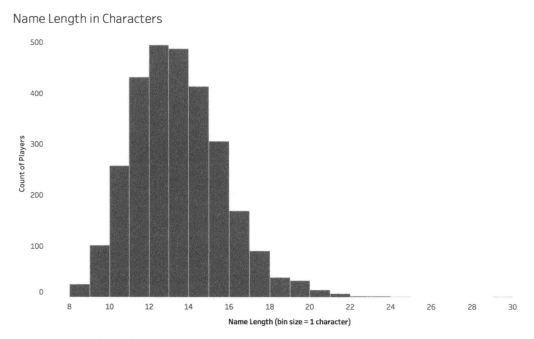

Name Length in Characters

FIGURE 5.10   Name length in characters.

than the tallest person ever to play *basketball* in the North American professional basketball league. (Manute Bol and Gheorghe Muresan were the tallest players to play in the NBA, and they both stood at 7'7".)

E. Multimodal Distribution: Player Weight

The fifth distribution to consider shows us how heavy football players are. Figure 5.11 is the three-humped, multimodal distribution.

Where does this odd shape come from? It comes from the fact that there are different positions on the field that require very different body types.

There are the very large players called "linemen" on both offense and defense who find themselves in a clash of titans seeking to control the middle of the field. There are the speedy and agile wide receivers on offense and their counterparts on defense in the

Player Weight

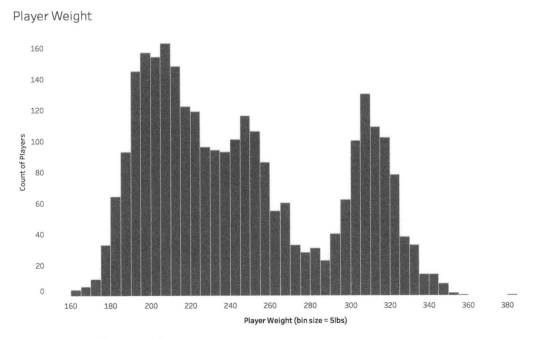

FIGURE 5.11 Player weight.

secondary who seek to get open and catch or defend a pass from the quarterback. And then there's everyone else. There are close to 1,000 players in each of these three groups.

If we break up the histogram in Figure 5.11 by these rough groups of positions, we see that the league indeed comprises different types of players in terms of weight (Figure 5.12).

Remember that the average weight of all players is 244.7 pounds. It's easy to see from the histograms above that this is a pretty typical weight for the "all other positions" category, but it's an incredibly uncommon weight for the other two groups, which, put together, comprise roughly two-thirds of the players in the league. So is 244 pounds "typical"? No, not really. At least not for all position groups.

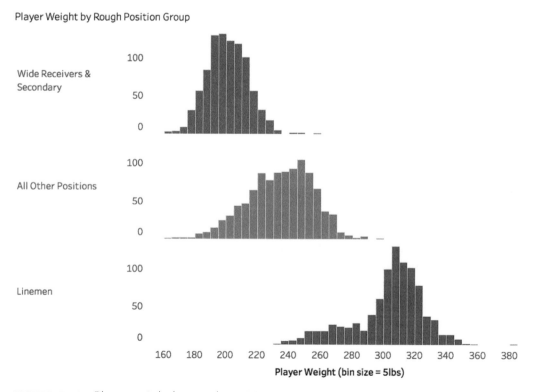

FIGURE 5.12 Player weight by rough position group.

So it is with distributions that have multiple modes, or humps in the shape of the distribution. The overall mean might map well to "typical" for one of the subgroups, or it might not map well to any of them. Without a doubt, there are subgroups in multimodal distributions for which the overall mean would be an incredibly unlikely value indeed.

F. Player Salary Cap Hit

I have saved the best distribution for last. If we look at how much money each player in the league makes in terms of the team's "cap hit" for that player – a technicality that factors in prorating of signing bonuses and such that we don't need to worry about too much here – then we noted earlier that on average, a player makes $1.5 million per year. The exact amount for 1,999 players in the 2017 season was $1.489 million.

Remember, the mean (aka "arithmetic average," aka just "average") is the "representative value" for the entire distribution. In other words, if we replaced each player's actual salary with the average salary of $1.489 million, then all of the owners put together would be on the hook for the exact same total amount of salary for the entire league of players, or around $2.97 billion.

Many, many players would be happy with that arrangement. If we look at the distribution in Figure 5.13 for salary cap hit, we see that the three largest bins – $0–$499K, $500K–$1M, and $1M–$1.5M – are pretty much at or below the average value.

In fact, a full 1,532 of the 1,999 players for whom I was able to find salary data for the 2017 season make less than the average salary. That's 76.6% of the players. The vast majority of players would be justifiably annoyed if you assumed they made around $1.5 million per year, and they'd be thrilled with a switch to the average.

But some players would be livid. Like Kirk Cousins, the quarterback whose cap hit in 2017 was almost $24 million. His mark in the histogram is the one way out there to the right. You can barely see it. He's the one who made 16 times the average player salary amount.

Salary Cap Hit

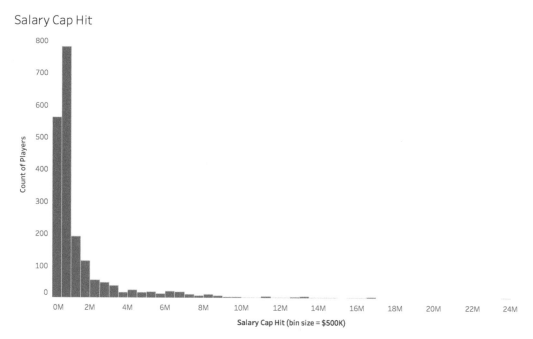

FIGURE 5.13   Salary cap hit.

If we try to evaluate this distribution using the standard deviation (σ), Cousins would be more than 10σ greater than the mean. If there was a player whose height was 10σ greater than the average height, that player would be 8′4″. To put that in perspective, the tallest person alive right now is a full 3 inches shorter than that at 8′1″.

And the standard deviation of salary? It's $2.25 million – so, larger than the mean itself, which is $1.489 million. As you can see, salary is a totally different type of distribution altogether. It's certainly not a uniform distribution, and it's not anything like a normal distribution.

It's called a power law distribution, and the thing is, it's everywhere in social sciences. Try to imagine the distribution of the number of followers for each social media account. There are a relatively small number of accounts with an enormous number of followers – millions and millions of followers each – and an incredibly long tail of accounts with just a few followers or less. This is true of so many things. Book sales, website visitors, music track listens on streaming services, movies. As humans, we focus a huge amount of our attention and we give a very large percentage of our money and adoration to a relatively small number of other humans and products. In so many things in human life, to the victor goes an insane portion of the spoils.

That's why power law distributions are often said to follow the Pareto rule, or the 80–20 rule: 80% of the spoils goes to 20% of the people. The numbers 80 and 20 aren't etched in stone, by the way, just an easy way of getting across the idea that a disproportionate amount of something is given to relatively few.

In the football player salary example, we're considering right now, for example, 80% of the salary in terms of cap hit would be claimed by the top 800 money earners in the league, or 40% of the entire league. A full half of the overall cap hit in the league went to 214 players, or just over 10% of the total league. If we plot the cumulative salary of each player, starting with the highest wage earners like Cousins to the left, and then adding the next player's salary to the total and so on, we see just how skewed this distribution is (Figure 5.14).

Contrast that with the cumulative distribution of player heights, where the tallest players like the aforementioned Nate Wozniak are placed to the far left (Figure 5.15).

It's almost a perfectly straight line. Here's another way to think about it. If you built a staircase where the height of each step was proportional to the height of each player, and the first step from the ground was for the tallest player and the last step at the top was for the shortest player, you'd hardly be able to see a difference at all if you looked at the whole staircase from a distance. On the other hand, if you did the same thing but you made each step proportional to the stack of bills each player makes? Yeah, you'd notice the difference all right – the staircase would bend dramatically like the arc above.

And think about it – we're only considering a population of people who play the exact same sport in the exact same league, and we

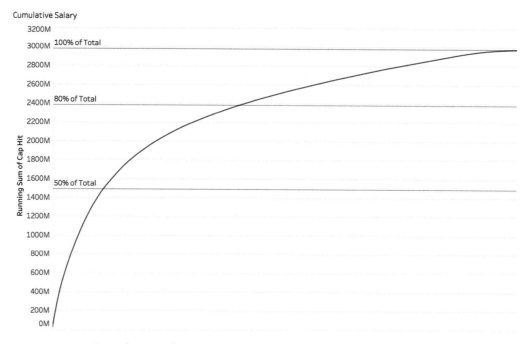

FIGURE 5.14 Cumulative salary.

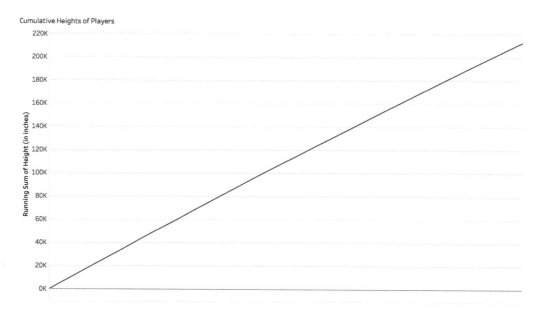

FIGURE 5.15 Cumulative heights of players.

still get astronomically higher than average values in the set. Imagine how much more variation we'd see if we considered a wider group – say, all athletes. Or even wider – all Americans. Or all citizens of planet earth. The distribution in income of all 7.53 billion people isn't anything like the distribution of those same individuals' heights, and it isn't anything like the distribution of the outcome of a single die roll if everyone took a turn and wrote down the number showing from 1 to 6.

These are all very different types of variation. But the pitfall – and it's a "humdinger" as my mom likes to say – is that we almost always think that "average" means "typical" for each one of them. It doesn't.

Pitfall 4B: Inferential Infernos

When we have data about all of the members of a population, such as the football league player data in the previous section, there's no need to make any inferences about the difference between groups within that population, because we're dealing with all of the data.

We don't have to infer which team has the tallest average player height, for example, because we can just compute average height for each team and then sort the teams in descending order. This is descriptive statistics, and we saw how even that activity can be tricky. (It was Pittsburgh, by the way.)

Many times, though, when we're working with data, it isn't feasible, practical, or cost effective to obtain data about every single one of the individual elements of a given population, so we have to collect data from samples, and make inferences about differences between groups. Here's where the trickiness increases by leaps and bounds.

There's a reason the census in the United States is decennial – meaning it only happens once every 10 years: it's very expensive and extremely difficult to attempt to count every single person in every single residential structure in the entire country, and such an undertaking is not without its sources of bias and error. The current budget request for the FY 2020 census is $6.3 billion.[6] That's not a cheap data collection program at all. Worthwhile? Sure. But not cheap.

Since most organizations don't have the resources of the U.S. federal government or billions of dollars of funding to undertake such an exhaustive initiative, they make decisions based on data taken from subsets of the population. A lot. But they don't always do it right.

Making inferences based on data from samples of the population is a particular stretch on the road to data heaven that is absolutely full of pitfalls, one after the other. It very well might be the most treacherous zone of all.

Here are some common examples in everyday life and business that involve using data taken from a subset of the population:

- Customer satisfaction: When companies seek to survey their customers, they know that many won't respond to their email survey, so it can be very difficult to get 100% feedback from an entire group of people who have purchased your product or service.
- Quality control: When engineers want to test whether products in manufacturing meet specifications, the tests can often be costly, and sometimes even destructive in nature (like determining tensile strength), so it wouldn't make financial or practical sense to test 100% of the parts.
- Clinical trials: Researching the efficacy of an experimental drug means researchers need to see whether a group of study participants who used the drug fared any better than another group in the study that took a placebo. Also, inferences are made about how the drug will affect patients who take it after it is released into the market.

---

[6] https://www2.census.gov/about/budget/census-fiscal-year-20-budget-infographic-2020-census.pdf.

These are just a few examples where statistical inference is required to make informed decisions. These are clearly important scenarios.

To start the discussion about how statistical inference can go awry, I'll relate some experience from early in my career. I started my career as a mechanical design engineer working in a high-volume automotive sensor factory that mostly produced pressure sensors for under-the-hood applications for cars and trucks. These sensors were being cranked out by the tens of thousands each and every shift, sometimes three shifts per day. Even tiny process or equipment changes could result in massive quality issues and costly scrap, with bins upon bins full of "out of spec" parts piling up in the back of the building. Poor quality was very hard to sweep under the rug.

In that environment, it was critical to study how small changes would impact the quality of the parts being produced. Let's say a vendor who produced one of the components used in the final assembly made a change to a manufacturing process as volumes increased, resulting in a shift of a critical dimension on a print such as a shaft diameter – even a shift that resulted in components that were still "in spec," or within the minimum and maximum allowable limits of the diameter, for example. How would this shift affect the overall performance of the manufacturing line? Would it perhaps affect some downstream quality assurance test in a negative way and cause fallout in production? How could the team know before creating batches upon batches of bad parts that would need to be thrown away?

Our quality engineers would perform an experiment – a qualification run – and they would obtain data from a set of sample parts that would make their way through the entire production line using the new components, and this data would be compared to data from parts made with the "old" components – the ones we used before the supplier made the change to their process.

These studies would require us to perform "null hypothesis statistical tests" such as Student's t-test, ANOVA, and chi-squared tests, among others. These tests are easy to compute, but they're tricky, and the concepts behind them are slippery and very easy to get wrong, even for experts.

So how do they work? For those of you well-grounded in statistics, you know this next part. But maybe not. Maybe you get it wrong from time to time, too, like I do.

The key to a null hypothesis statistical test is the null hypothesis – the scenario in which there's actually no difference between the groups being tested. Since random samples drawn from a population won't have the exact same mean and standard deviation all the time, some variation in these statistics is to be expected. How does that amount of likely variation compare with the actual difference observed in the experiment?

Hypothesis tests start with the assumption that the null hypothesis is true, and then they seek to determine how likely it would be to observe differences in sample statistics, such as the mean and standard deviation, *at least as great as what was actually observed in the experiment*, taking into account the number of samples, the size of the difference measured, and the amount of variation observed in each group. This is similar to the "presumption of innocence" in courts of law, but not exactly the same, because there's no "proving" the null hypothesis innocent or guilty. It's just a probabilistic assessment.

That's a mouthful, though, so it's no wonder people get it wrong. The key output of the null hypothesis test is the p-value. Much has been written about the much maligned and often defended p-value in many fields of study. The p-value just tells you the probability of seeing a difference at least as big as the one observed in the experiment, assuming the null hypothesis is true and there's no difference in the groups being tested. The p-value doesn't prove or disprove anything – a high p-value doesn't prove that the null hypothesis is true, and a low p-value doesn't prove that it's false. In practice, though, that's how people often think of it and use it.

There are a number of pitfalls in play here:

- Simply computing the difference in mean between the different groups and assuming any difference you see is statistically significant, ignoring the statistical probabilities altogether. We'll call this the **"p-what? pitfall."**

- Getting a p-value that's low by sheer chance and therefore rejecting the null hypothesis when it's actually true is the **"Type 1 pitfall."** In other words, you assume there's a statistically significant difference between the groups when they're basically cut from the same cloth.

- Getting a p-value that's high means you can fall into the **"Type 2 pitfall"** by failing to reject the null hypothesis when it's actually false.

- Misunderstanding the concept of statistical significance altogether, you get a low p-value in an experiment and then you run around the building waving a piece of paper and claiming to everyone who will listen that you have *definitive proof* that the null hypothesis is dead wrong, because MATH! Let's call this pitfall "**p is for proof, right?**"

- Running a test in which you collect data on many, many different variables, you blindly compute p-values for dozens upon dozens of comparisons, and lo and behold, you find a couple of low p-values in the mix. You don't bother confirming it or asking others to replicate your results. You just sit back and breathe a sigh of relief that you found a low p-value and thank the stats gods that now you'll have something to write about. We'll call this pitfall "**p is for publish, right?**"

- You confuse the notion of practical significance and statistical significance, and you conduct a huge clinical study with thousands and thousands of patients, some taking an experimental drug and others a placebo. You get a p-value of <0.0001 for your key factor – lifespan – but you forget to look at the size of the difference between the means. The difference is vanishingly small, and test subjects can expect to live 2 days longer in total. Of course, this pitfall is called the **"p is for practical, right?"**

These are just a handful of pitfalls that null hypothesis testing can cause us to fall into, which is at least part of the reason why a number of scientists, researchers, and statisticians are ditching the procedure altogether in favor of Bayesian methods such as the Bayesian information criterion.[7]

Pitfall 4C: Slippery Sampling

On some level, we all know that the data we're using to make conclusions about the world isn't perfect. We know that there remains some uncertainty about everything the human mind considers. From survey results to clinical studies to engineering bridges, there's always some error involved in the numbers. We tend to neglect this uncertainty, and lead ourselves and others astray as a result.

Case in point: fish labels.

On Fish Labels

When a nonprofit published the findings of their seafood labeling fraud investigation in February 2013, the results were shocking: "more than 1,200 seafood samples taken from 674 retail outlets in 21 states" yielded a disturbing trend – over 33% of DNA samples didn't match their label. You can read the news on the nonprofit's website.[8]

I first heard about the study while driving to work in Seattle after coming back from the Tapestry Conference in Nashville. At Tapestry, we had discussed uncertainty following Jonathan Corum's keynote, so the topic was fresh in my mind.

An Inferential Leap

Northwest Public Radio had the following to say about the study in an article that is no longer available on their site: "Seattle and Portland are among the best cities in the country to buy fish that is accurately labeled." On the surface, it made perfect sense. Seattle and Portland are coastal cities with robust fishing industries. Of course

---

[7] https://www.ejwagenmakers.com/2007/pValueProblems.pdf.
[8] https://oceana.org/reports/oceana-study-reveals-seafood-fraud-nationwide.

they'd be better than cities like Austin or Denver. The NPR article went on to state that the lower rates may be due to "consumer awareness about seafood in Seattle." Flattering.

For fun, I thought I'd take a deeper look, so I found the full report online.[9] Let's take a look at the report to see what can be said about Seattle and Portland, if anything. The charts that follow are my own creations from the raw data available in the report.

If we just look at the overall percent of samples mislabeled by city, we find Seattle and Portland among the best, along with another famous North American fishing hub, Boston (Figure 5.16).

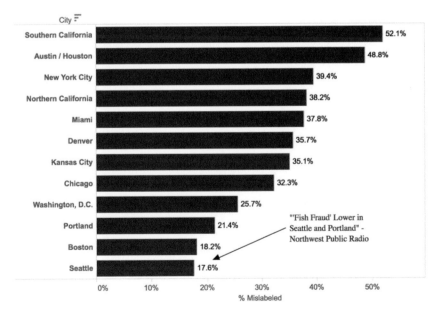

FIGURE 5.16 Mislabeled fish, misleading bars.

_____

[9] http://oceana.org/sites/default/files/reports/National_Seafood_Fraud_Testing_Results_FINAL.pdf.

Case closed then, right? If this were all we were given, we'd make the same inferences as Northwest Public Radio. But were the cities sampled properly to make this statement?

Samples were taken from three types of retail outlets: grocery stores, restaurants, and sushi venues. Here are the results by each city and retail category pairing. Mislabeled samples are red bars, and correctly labeled samples are blue bars (Figure 5.17).

The first thing I noticed is that there are some pretty small sample sizes in there, once you break it down into cities and retail categories. Yes, there may be "more than 1,200" samples overall, but 12 samples from restaurants in the Austin/Houston area? And 9 samples from sushi joints in Kansas City?

Fish Mislabeling by City & Outlet

From 2010-12, Oceana conducted DNA testing of various types of fish in U.S. cities and determined whether the food was **mislabeled** or correctly labeled. Overall 33% of the 1,215 samples were mislabeled, with **Sushi** mislabeled most often. Seattle came out on top, but did Oceana's sampling plan allow for city-to-city comparison?

Data Source | Oceana.org   Feb 2013

FIGURE 5.17   Fish mislabeling by city and outlet.

If we look at the data they provide, we can see that sushi venues seemed to yield the poorest results, with over 73% mislabeled across all cities (some of the sushi mislabeling was due to "foreign name translation" – e.g. not all types of fish called "yellowfish" in Japan meet the FDA classification).

But the other thing we notice is that very different amounts of sushi were collected in each city. In fact, no sushi was collected in Boston at all.

Breaking Down the Mix

Figure 5.18 shows a breakdown of the mix of each retail category in each city's sample set (thickness of the bars is proportional to mislabeling – thicker meaning a higher mislabeling rate).

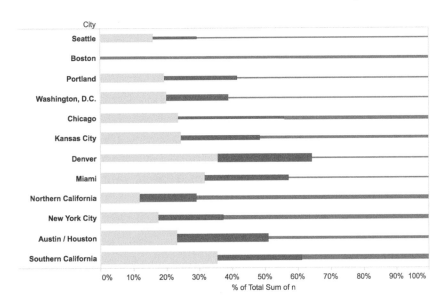

FIGURE 5.18 A fishy sample platter.

So, relatively low amounts of sushi samples were sampled in Seattle, Portland, and Boston. Of the samples in Seattle, 16% were sushi, while over 35% of the samples in Southern California were sushi, by comparison.

This organization didn't follow a stratified sampling plan when they collected their 1,214 samples and as a result, the overall mislabeling rates from each city really aren't apples-to-apples comparisons. This doesn't mean their study is meaningless; it just means that comparing the *overall* rates between cities isn't all that valid. It would be like comparing average human heights in each city and including way more children in one city's sample set than the others. It's just not fair dice.

Comparing Like-to-Like

Okay, since we can't really compare the overall rates, what if we just compare the cities within each retail category: so grocery stores to grocery stores, restaurants to restaurants, and sushi to sushi?

Even though a relatively high number of samples were taken overall, the sample sizes start getting fairly small when you look at each city/category combination, so we should add error bars to the mislabeling rates. This is a case for the binomial proportion confidence interval.[10] There are a number of different ways to compute this interval, but for now we'll stick with the normal approximation that we all learned in college. Figure 5.19 shows the breakdown of mislabeling rates, with uncertainty taken into account.

This data visualization tells a very different story. Notice that not every city is included in this chart. That's because in some cases, there weren't enough samples to satisfy the requirements of the normal approximation ($n*p>5$ and $n*(1-p)>5$), so I filtered these cases out of the chart. Kansas City drops out altogether, for example – not enough samples in KC (19, 9, and 9) to say much of anything about labeling there.

---

[10] https://en.wikipedia.org/wiki/Binomial_proportion_confidence_interval.

Mislabeled Fish, with Error Bars

When confidence intervals are taken into consideration, it becomes clear that we can't say as much about which city is better and which is worse, even within retail categories.

Confidence level
0.95 ▼

Retail Category
Sushi ▼

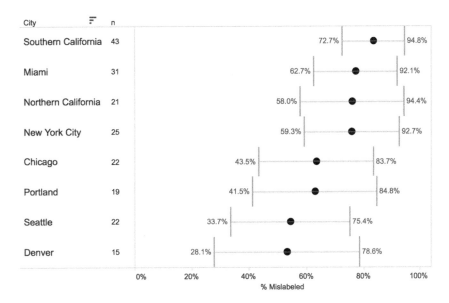

Data Source | Oceana.org

Feb 2013

FIGURE 5.19 Mislabeled fish, with error bars.

What can we say about the different cities? Here's what we can (and can't) say based on a 95% confidence interval (ignoring the difference in the types of fish samples collected at each place):

- We don't have enough evidence to say whether any city is better or worse than any other in sushi mislabeling.
- The probability is high that restaurants in Chicago overall had lower mislabeling rates than restaurants in Northern California.
- The probability is high that grocery stores in Seattle had lower mislabeling than in both California (Southern and Northern) and New York.

So some comparisons can be made between cities, just not all that many. In the end, Seattleites can take consolation in the fact that the fish in their grocery stores is probably labeled more accurately than in California and New York, and perhaps this is even partly due to their seafood IQ.

If their tests are to be trusted, and if they can be replicated, then this nonprofit revealed widespread mislabeling of fish in the United States – that much can't be denied. But a massive inferential leap was made in reporting the story. Looking at the numbers through the lens of statistics allows us to make more accurate statements about the findings.

Yes, this involves much more work than simply taking the over-all mislabeled rate and slapping it into a map or bar chart. And yes, uncertainty can be annoying. But we are falling into a pitfall and deceiving ourselves and others if we don't understand how our sampling plan and the confidence bands of the rates affect our ability to draw probabilistic conclusions about the world in which we live.

Embracing uncertainty just may mean the difference between truth and fiction, and we wouldn't want fishy results, now would we?

Pitfall 4D: Insensitivity to Sample Size

If you deal with numbers at all and haven't yet read *Thinking, Fast and Slow* by Nobel Prize winner Daniel Kahneman,[11] I highly recommend you read it. It's a fascinating book about cognitive biases and "heuristics" (rules of thumb) in decision making. In it he refers to an article by Howard Wainer and Harris L. Zwerling called "Evidence That Smaller Schools Do Not Improve Student Achievement" that talks about kidney cancer rates.[12]

Kidney cancer is a relatively rare form of cancer, accounting for only about 4% of all new adult cancer cases. According to the American Cancer Society, an estimated 73,820 cases out of 1,762,450 total new

---

[11] https://us.macmillan.com/books/9780374533557.
[12] https://journals.sagepub.com/doi/abs/10.1177/003172170608800411?-journalCode=pdka.

cases in 2019 in the United States will be kidney and renal pelvis cancer cases.[13] If you look at kidney cancer rates by county in the U.S. an interesting pattern emerges, as he describes on page 109 of his book:

> *The counties in which the incidence of kidney cancer is lowest are mostly rural, sparsely populated, and located in traditionally Republican states in the Midwest, the South, and the West.*

What do you make of this? He goes on to list some of the reasons people have come up with in an attempt to rationalize this fact, such as the ideas that residents of rural counties have access to fresh food or that they are exposed to less air pollution. Did these explanations come to your mind, too? He then points out the following:

> *Now consider the counties in which the incidence of kidney cancer is highest. These ailing counties tend to be mostly rural, sparsely populated, and located in traditionally Republican states in the Midwest, the South, and the West.*

Again, people come up with various theories to explain this fact: rural counties have relatively high poverty rates, high-fat diet, or lack of access to medication.

But wait – what's going on here? Rural counties have both the highest and the lowest kidney cancer rates? What gives?

This is a great example of a bias known as "insensitivity to sample size."[14] It goes like this: when we deal with data, we don't take into account sample size when we think about probability. These rural counties have relatively few people, and as such, they are more likely to have either very high or very low incidence rates. Why? Because the variance of the mean is proportional to the sample size. The smaller the sample, the greater the variance. There is, of course, rigorous mathematical proof for this fact if you're interested in following the steps.[15]

---

[13] https://cancerstatisticscenter.cancer.org/#!/.
[14] https://en.wikipedia.org/wiki/Insensitivity_to_sample_size.
[15] https://newonlinecourses.science.psu.edu/stat414/node/167/.

In looking into this matter further, I managed to find kidney cancer rate figures[16] as well as the population data for each U.S. county,[17] and I created an interactive dashboard (Figure 5.20) to visually illustrate the point that Kahneman, Wainer, and Zwerlink are making quite clearly in words.

Notice a few things in the dashboard. In the choropleth (filled) map, the darkest orange counties (high rates relative to the overall U.S. rate) and the darkest blue counties (low rates relative to the overall U.S. rate) are often right next to each other.

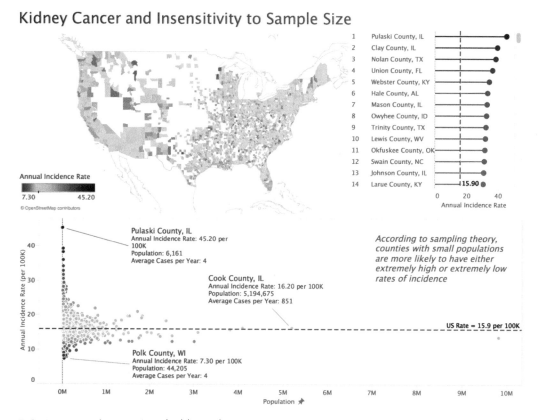

FIGURE 5.20   Interactive dashboard.

[16] https://statecancerprofiles.cancer.gov/map/map.withimage.php?99&001&072&00&0&01&0&1&6&0#results.
[17] https://seer.cancer.gov/popdata/.

Furthermore, notice how in the scatterplot below the map, the marks form a funnel shape, with less populous counties (to the left) more likely to deviate from the reference line (the overall U.S. rate), and more populous counties like Chicago, L.A., and New York more likely to be close to the overall reference line.

One final observation: if you hover over a county with a small population in the interactive online version, you'll notice that the average number of cases per year is extremely low, sometimes 4 cases or fewer. A small deviation – even just 1 or 2 cases – in a subsequent year will shoot a county from the bottom of the list to the top, or vice versa.

Other Examples

Where else does "insensitivity to sample size" come up? An interesting example is the notion of "streaks" in sports, which can often be simply a "clustering illusion."[18] How does this work? We observe a limited sample of a player's overall performance and notice temporary periods of greatness. But we should expect to see such streaks for even mediocre players. Remember Linsanity?

Similarly, small samples make some rich and others poor in the world of gambling. You may have a good day at the tables, but if you keep playing, eventually the house will win.

So what do we do about it? How do we make sure we don't fall into the pitfall known as "insensitivity to sample size"?

1. Be aware of any sampling involved in the data we are analyzing.

2. Understand that the smaller the sample size, the more likely we will see a rate or statistic that deviates significantly from the population.

3. Before forming theories about why a particular sample deviates from the population in some way, first consider that it may just be noise and chance.

---

[18] https://en.wikipedia.org/wiki/Clustering_illusion.

4. Visualize the rate or statistic associated with groups of varying size in a scatterplot. If you see the telltale funnel shape, then you know not to be fooled.

The point of the original article by Wainer and Zwerling is that smaller schools are apt to yield extreme test scores by virtue of the fact that there aren't enough students in small schools to "even out" the scores. A random cluster of extremely good (or bad) performers can sway a small school's scores. At a very big school a few bad results will still affect the overall mean, but not nearly as much.

Here's another way to think of it. Lost Springs, Wyoming, is a town with a population of one (Figure 5.21). If Daniel Kahneman ever

FIGURE 5.21   The traffic sign welcoming drivers to Lost Springs, Wyoming.
Source: Wikimedia Commons. Public domain.

moved to Lost Springs, Wyoming, then half of the town's population would be Nobel Prize winners. And if you think that moving there would increase your chances of winning the Nobel Prize, or that it's "in the water" or some other such reason, then you're suffering from a severe case of insensitivity to sample size.

These are just a handful of statistical slipups, a type of pitfall on the road to data paradise that is particularly nasty and easy to fall into. Entire books have been written on this topic, and more really should be said for this chapter to be complete. But I'll stop here and we'll move on to other topics worthy of our consideration.

Chapter Six

Pitfall 5: Analytical Aberrations

"Data is a tool for enhancing intuition."

—*Hilary Mason*

How We Analyze Data

What is the purpose of collecting data? People gather and store data for at least three different reasons that I can discern. One reason is that they want to build an arsenal of evidence with which to prove a point or defend an agenda that they already had to begin with. This path is problematic for obvious reasons, and yet we all find ourselves traveling on it from time to time.

Another reason people collect data is that they want to feed it into an artificial intelligence algorithm to automate some process or carry out some task. This purpose involves a set of activities that I haven't really included in this book. But it, too, is fraught with pitfall after pitfall, on which I hope to write at some point in the future.

A third reason is that they might be collecting data in order to compile information to help them better understand their situation, to answer questions they have in their mind, and to unearth new questions that they didn't think to ask.

This last purpose is what we call data analysis, or analytics.

Pitfall 5A: The Intuition/Analysis False Dichotomy

Some years ago I saw a television commercial for Business Intelligence (BI) software in which a customer being interviewed had the following to say:

> *We used to use intuition; now we use analytics.*

In other words, we're being asked to believe that the business owner was able to make progress by *replacing* decision making using intuition with decision making using analytics.

The statement didn't sit well with me, so I immediately tweeted the following:

> *Software ad: "We used to use intuition; now we use analytics." This is the wrong mindset. One should complement, not replace, the other.*

Working in the BI industry for many years, I heard similar attacks on human intuition from many different sides, and I don't agree with it at all. Here's my feeling on the topic in a nutshell: in a world awash with data, human intuition is actually more valuable than ever. Briefly, human intuition is the spark plug that makes the analytics engine run.

Intuition Wasn't Always a Byword

Contrast the commercial's negative attitude toward human intuition with Albert Einstein's rather glowing appraisal (Figure 6.1).

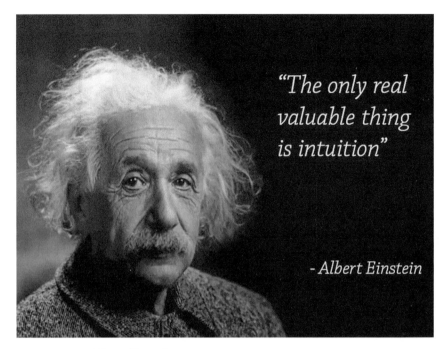

FIGURE 6.1   Albert Einstein.
Source: https://pixabay.com/photos/albert-einstein-portrait-1933340/.

Without a doubt, it would be hard to come up with a more positive statement about intuition than this.

So, which is it? Is human intuition a faulty and antiquated decision-making tool, in dire need of replacement with something better, or is it the only valuable thing there is?

Before we go any further, we should define the terms. The *Oxford English Dictionary* defines intuition as follows:

> *The ability to understand something immediately, without the need for conscious reasoning.*

It comes from the Latin root word *intueri,* meaning to look at or gaze upon. Thus, the etymology of the word links it with the human visual system. Sight and intuition both occur instantaneously and effortlessly. Both can also mislead, of which more later. With intuition, as with sight, the awareness comes before any logical explanation.

The link between intuition and sight is often a very literal one. In social situations, we intuitively sense other people's emotions when we first lay eyes on their facial expressions (Figure 6.2).

FIGURE 6.2   Facial expressions.
Source: J. Campbell Cory, *The Cartoonist's Art* (Chicago: Tumbo Company, 1912).

And with abstract representations of data, we spot the marks that have certain unusual attributes in an intuitive way – that is, we notice them without having to think about it. We call these attributes "pre-attentive." Noticing them doesn't take effort; it's as if it happens to us. Figure 6.3 shows two versions of the same scatterplot, which plots the top scoring players in the North American professional hockey league in terms of the number of shots they took on net and the number of goals they scored over their career (for those who played after shots on net began being collected as a statistic).

The shapes in the scatterplot are determined by the position of the player. If I wanted to determine how many left wing players (indicated by arrows, or triangles, pointing to the left) are present in the view,

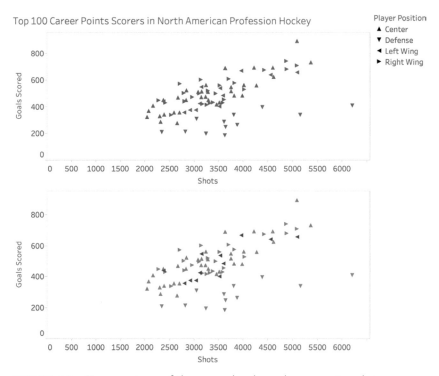

FIGURE 6.3   Two versions of the same hockey player scatterplot.

it would be very time-consuming and error prone for me to use the top version of the graph. With this version, I need to scan the shapes, find each left arrow, keep its location in my mind so that I don't double count it, and hope I don't miss any. If I use the bottom version of the graph, however, answering the question becomes quite simple, and I can have a high degree of confidence that the answer is 12.

So there is a component of our intuition that we engage when we read charts and graphs. Similarly, we can feel a compelling sense of confidence in a specific situation about what is happening and why, as well as what's going to happen in the future, and what we should do about it now. This is what's commonly meant when someone says a person has a great intuition about a specific field.

Intuition is commonly contrasted with reason, "the power of the mind to think, understand, and form judgments by a process of logic." Logic, in turn, involves "strict principles of validity." And analytics is "information resulting from the systematic analysis of data or statistics."

To make the best decisions in business and in life, we need to be adept at many different forms of thinking, including intuition, and we need to know how to incorporate many different types of inputs, including numerical data and statistics (analytics). Intuition and analytics don't have to be seen as mutually exclusive at all. In fact, they can be viewed as complementary.

Let me give some examples of how intuition provides the spark for the analytical process.

Five Reasons Why Intuition Still Matters
1. Knowing WHY any of it matters in the first place
Any process has an almost infinite number of variables that could be tracked and analyzed. On which should we spend our time?

Knowing where to start can be a problem, especially if we know very little about the subject we're dealing with.

One school of thought goes something like this: collect data on everything and let an algorithm tell you which to pay attention to.

Sorry, I don't buy it.

First, not even the NSA collects data on "everything." I guarantee you a filter has been applied to narrow the set of inputs. God may have counted every hair on your head, but I seriously doubt any-one else has.

Second, while data mining algorithms can discover notable pat-terns in huge data sets, only human intuition can discern between the useful patterns and the useless ones. They get their very "use-fulness" from our goals and values.

2. Knowing WHAT the data is telling us (and what it's not telling us)
Once we pick data to collect and metrics to analyze, what do the numbers tell us? We talked about preattentive attributes briefly – via data visualization, our intuition can be put to good use inter-preting the important 1s and 0s in the databases we've meticu-lously built.

Using intuition in this way isn't a perfect process though. Just as we might recoil from a garden hose that our instincts tell us is a snake, we can see signals in data that aren't really there. Alternatively, we can miss really important signals that are there. Just because intuition doesn't work perfectly, though, doesn't mean it should be discarded. We just need to hone our intuition for working with num-bers, and we need to distrust it somewhat.

3. Knowing WHERE to look next
Jonas Salk, the American medical researcher who developed the first polio vaccine, had the following to say about intuition in his book *Anatomy of Reality: Merging of Intuition and Reason:*

Intuition will tell the thinking mind where to look next.

He made a discovery that has saved the lives of countless people in the world, and he chalked up an important part of his success to intuition. Often the best outcome of an interaction with data is that we sense another, even better question to ask. And the process iterates. The realization of the next place to look can form in our mind like an intuitive spark. The light bulb analogy applies.

4. Knowing WHEN to stop looking and take action

For many types of questions or problems, we could continue to search for a solution ad nauseum. Think of a chess game. What's the "best move" to make at a given point in the game? Russian chess Grandmaster Garry Kasparov understood something about this question, as stated in his book *How Life Imitates Chess* (Figure 6.4).

There comes a point in time when it's best to stop analyzing and make a move. Knowing when we've arrived at this point is a function of intuition. If we don't have this intuitive switch, we can suffer from "analysis paralysis," and then we go nowhere. We've all been there. Kasparov went on to say:

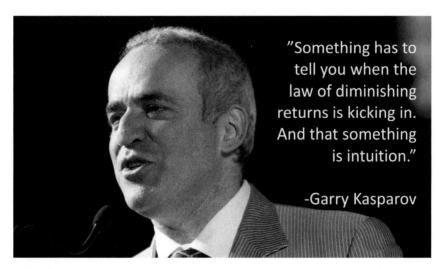

FIGURE 6.4   Quote from Garry Kasparov's book *How Life Imitates Chess*.
Source: https://commons.wikimedia.org/wiki/File:Garry_Kasparov_IMG_0130.JPG. Used under CC BY-SA 3.0.

The things we usually think of as advantages – having more time to think and analyze, having more information at our disposal – can short-circuit what matters even more: our intuition.

5. Knowing WHO *needs to hear, and* HOW *to get through to them*
A key part of the data discovery process is communicating our findings with others. We can use our intuition to choose the best message, channel, venue, visualization types, aesthetic elements, timing, tone, pace, and so on. If we have a deep understanding of our audience, we will intuitively know what will get through to them, and what will fall on deaf ears. When we get it right, it can be a wonder to behold. Think Hans Rosling.

Who is Hans Rosling? He is the late Swedish physician, world health statistician, and co-founder of the Gapminder Foundation. He delivered a TED talk titled "The best stats you've ever seen" that has been viewed over 13.5 million times to date.[1] In it, he brings data to life like many of us had never seen before. He used an animated bubble chart to dispel many myths about the state of health and development across the world, enthusiastically describing the movement of the country circles across the screen more like a sportscaster calling a horse race than an academic describing statistical trends.

I got a chance to meet Dr. Rosling at a software conference in Seattle in 2016 where he was delivering a keynote about the changing face of the world's population. What object did he use to illustrate the growth projection by age group? Toilet paper, of course.[2] In a peak moment for my career, it was my job to go to the local drug store and buy Hans his toilet paper. It's all downhill from there, people.

Crafting the communication is a creative process, and human intuition will need to be tapped to do it well. Rosling understood that.

So there you have it: not only does data not replace intuition and render it irrelevant, but intuition is actually the thing that makes data

---

[1] https://www.ted.com/talks/hans_rosling_shows_the_best_stats_you_ve_ever_seen?language=en.
[2] https://www.youtube.com/watch?v=dnmDc-oR9eA.

of any value at all. Take out intuition, and you take out why, what, where, when, who, and how. Sure, data may be the "new oil," but human intuition is the spark plug that ignites the fuel in the engine.

For the reasons outlined above, I don't believe that human intuition will ever be rendered obsolete. No matter how smart our algorithms get, no matter how sophisticated our tools or methods, the intuitive "spark" in the human mind will always be the key element in our thoughts, in our decisions, and in our discoveries. Data and analytics can be the fuel lit by these sparks, and they can provide a way to make sure we're headed in the right direction, but they can't replace human intuition. Not the way I understand it, anyway.

I don't think the creators of the commercial would necessarily disagree with this point of view, so it likely comes down to semantics. Maybe the business owner in the commercial should have said, "We used to rely on intuition alone, now we combine it with analytics to make even better decisions." Slightly less snappy, I know. But at least intuition doesn't get thrown under the bus.

Pitfall 5B: Exuberant Extrapolations

While data analysis is often primarily concerned with understanding what has taken place in the past, people often think of "analytics" as the application of tools and techniques to use data in order to make decisions about the future. That involves predicting what's going to happen next, and how actions we take and changes we set in motion are likely to affect future trends.

But predicting what's going to happen in the future can be risky business, and the analytical process of forecasting is fraught with hazards and pitfalls galore. That's not to say we shouldn't attempt to do it, but rather that we should do so with humility and a sense of humor about it, with our pitfall radar on full power. It helps to be aware of our often wildly inaccurate "data-driven" prognostications. Seeing how often we and others have gotten it wrong can serve as a healthy reminder to us.

Let's consider the problem we run into when we extrapolate trends into the future. One remarkable way that our world has changed over the course of the past half century is that people born in every single country are expected to live a lot longer now than those born in the 1960s.

For example, if we look at life expectancy in both North and South Korea through the 1960s and 1970s, we see that life expectancy started that period at around 50 years of age to the mid-60s. That is, people born in both sections of the Korean peninsula in 1960 were expected to live to around 50 years of age, and those born a decade and a half later in both places were expected to live to around 65 years of age (Figure 6.5).

I call this a "very steady increase" because linear regression trend-lines for both countries, shown in the plot as dashed lines, have p-values of less than 0.0001, and coefficients of determination, R^2, above 0.95, meaning that the change in the x variable (Year)

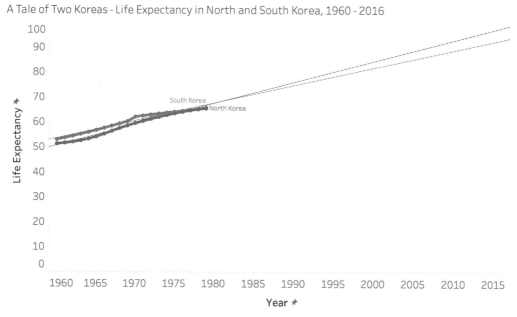

FIGURE 6.5   A tale of two Koreas: life expectancy in North and South Korea, 1960–2016.

accounts for a very high percentage of the variation observed in the y value (Life Expectancy). In other words, a straight line that minimizes the vertical distance between each data point and the line comes close to touching all of the points.

An even simpler way to say it? The data points for each series come really close to forming a straight line.

If someone in 1980 were to have relied solely on the linear nature of this 20-year time series to predict the life expectancies of both North and South Koreans who would be born 35 years into the future, they would have come up with life expectancies of 96 years for North Korea and 92 years for South Korea in the year 2015.

Of course, that's not what we really see, and this shouldn't surprise anyone. The reasons are obvious. First, because we can reason that the life expectancy of our species, even though it may increase in a linear fashion for some period of time, can't continue increasing at the same rate indefinitely. The data will start to hit a natural ceiling, because people don't live forever. Where is the ceiling, exactly? No one knows for sure. But if we extend the series ahead to the end of our own current century, people born on the Korean peninsula can expect to live for around 170 years. Not likely, and no one is saying that.

But that's not the only reason why our 1980s friend's prediction would have been way off. Take a look at the way the actual trendlines played out over the course of the past 35 years, leaving us where we are at present with life expectancies of around 82 for South Korea and 71 for North Korea (Figure 6.6).

While life expectancy of those born in South Korea continued to increase in a highly linear fashion ($R^2 = 0.986$), we can see that it's starting to bend downward and take on an expected nonlinear shape as it approaches some unknown asymptote.

But the case of North Korea is quite different. A very notable shift occurred on the north side of the peninsula, and life expectancy

A Tale of Two Koreas - Life Expectancy in North and South Korea, 1960 - 2016

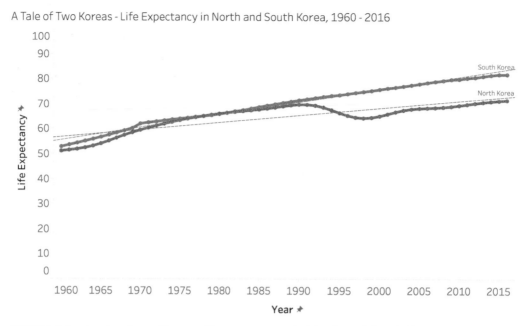

FIGURE 6.6 A tale of two Koreas: life expectancy in North and South Korea, 1960–2016.

actually dropped by 5 years during the 1990s as inhabitants in that country struggled with poor food availability and lack of access to other critical resources. Perhaps some people in 1980 had reason to be concerned about developing conditions in North Korea, but how would they have factored that knowledge into their forecast?

Sometimes, the forecast works out fairly nicely. In the case of Brazil, for example, growth in life expectancy has continued to be highly linear since 1960. Extrapolating the 1960 to 1975 trend in a linear fashion, we would've predicted a life expectancy of around 79 in Brazil by 2015. The actual life expectancy of Brazilians born in 2015 was 75. Not exactly Nostradamus-level, but not that bad, either.

Other times, though, it doesn't work out very nicely at all. In the case of China, for example, a linear extrapolation from 1975 would've produced a wild and unlikely prediction of 126 years for the life expectancy of people born in that country by 2015. Of course, the dramatic increases seen in the 1960s weren't sustained over the rest of the latter half of the twentieth century, and life expectancy for people born in China in 2015 was 76 years. (See Figure 6.7.)

The case of life expectancy in China shines the spotlight on one other area of caution when we fit equations to empirical data. Often we fit many different mathematical models to a data series, and we take the one with the closest fit, or the coefficient of determination closest to 1.0, regardless of what that model implies.

It turns out that the slight "S-shaped" curve in life expectancy in China between 1960 and the early 1970s follows a polynomial equation incredibly closely. Fitting a polynomial curve to the data yields a coefficient of determination, R^2, of 0.999899. It's really remarkable how close the data comes to a perfect polynomial equation. It actually makes me wonder how it was obtained.

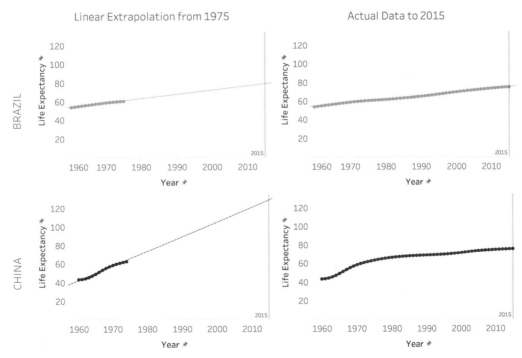

FIGURE 6.7   Linear extrapolation from 1975.

Setting that aside, take a look at the curve in Figure 6.8, zoomed in to see the shape and the model in more detail.

It doesn't take a genius to figure out that this model is even less useful for predicting future life expectancies than a linear one. It produces a completely nonsensical forecast, with life expectancies crashing to 0 and even becoming negative in a matter of a decade and a half.

It's actually pretty lucky for us when a model that fits the data so well turns out to be quite outrageous. It's as if there's a pitfall in the road, but it has a huge warning sign with bright flashing lights right in front of it. If we fall into that one, we're not really paying very close attention at all.

This has been a fun exercise in comparing a hypothetical extrapolation made by a fictional, unwitting analyst in the past with how things actually turned out. In this scenario, we have the benefit of the subsequent data points to see how extrapolation would have resulted in better accuracy in some countries than in others.

Life expectancy of people born in China, 1960 - 1972

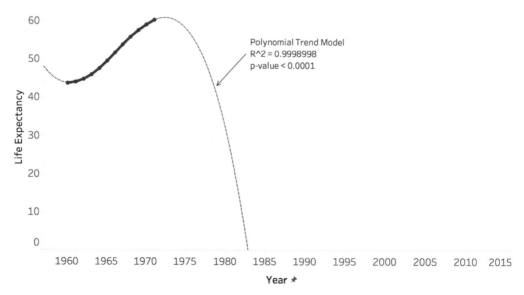

FIGURE 6.8   Life expectancy of people born in China, 1960–1972.

Sometimes we're not looking beyond existing data points, we're looking between them. That's the case for the next section, where we look at interpolations.

Pitfall 5C: Ill-Advised Interpolations

Any collection of time-series data involves a decision about sampling rate – the number of samples taken in a given unit of time. It's more commonly considered in signal processing and sound waves, where rates are measured in kilohertz (kHz) or thousands of samples per second, but it's a relevant factor to consider in any time-based data set. How often will data be collected? How much time will pass between each successive measurement? When we analyze or visualize the data, at what level of aggregation will we base our inquiry?

Let's continue using the same World Bank life expectancy data set to illustrate the impact of this choice on a macro scale – dealing with data on an annual basis.

The slopegraph is a popular way to visualize change over time. With a slopegraph, we simply connect the data from one period of time to the data from another, future period of time using a straight line. If we select seven specific countries and create a slopegraph showing how much life expectancy increased in each country in 1960 as opposed to 2015, we get the visual in Figure 6.9.

If you stop and think about it, we have just created an infinite number of brand new, fictional data points – the limitless number of points that lie on the line drawn between the two values. And what's the key takeaway from this fabrication? All countries increased in life expectancy between 1960 and 2015. It's not wrong to say that, by the way. It's a simple fact.

But it's woefully incomplete.

Let's see what happens when we add the annual values between these two years – over half a century of data about life expectancy. How does the story change? See Figure 6.10.

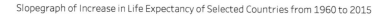

Slopegraph of Increase in Life Expectancy of Selected Countries from 1960 to 2015

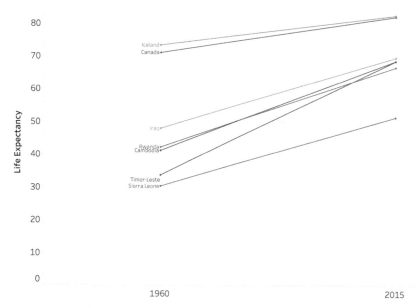

FIGURE 6.9 Slopegraph of increase in life expectancy.

Timeline of Change in Life Expectancy of Selected Countries between 1960 and 2015

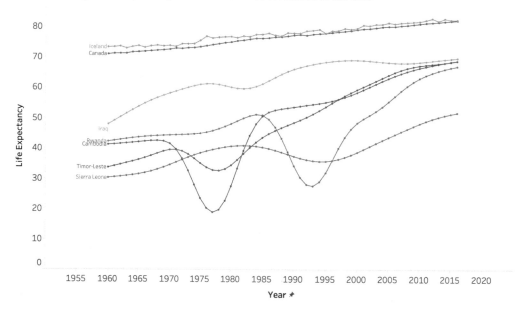

FIGURE 6.10 Timeline of change in life expectancy.

This visual tells a very different story, doesn't it? No longer missing are the tragic periods of war in Cambodia, Timor-Leste, Sierra Leone, and Rwanda. Yes, these countries saw dramatic increases in life expectancy over the course of the 55 years of time shown here. But they had to overcome massive bloodshed to get there. Life expectancy in Cambodia dropped to under 20 years of age in 1977 and 1978, the year I was born. The slopegraph fails miserably by completely omitting this story. It doesn't come close to telling us the full story.

Iraq is an interesting case, as well. The story that is missing from the slopegraph is that life expectancy in that country has hardly increased at all since the mid-1990s. Babies born in Iraq in 1995 were expected to live to 68 or 69 years of age, and the same can be said for babies born there in 2015. Two decades of stagnation. You don't see that in the slopegraph.

Finally, the comparison between Canada and Iceland is a technical one, but interesting all the same. In the slopegraph, it looks like these countries more or less follow each other closely. And they do. But if you compare how they look in the full timeline, you'll see that Iceland's line is somewhat jagged, with lots of small year-to-year noise, whereas Canada's line is much smoother. What's going on there? I'm not quite sure, but I can surmise that it has something to do with the way each country estimates and reports on life expectancy each year, and perhaps also the size of the population of each country. Clearly, they have different procedures, different ways of calculating and estimating this metric, different methods.

Does that matter? Maybe, and maybe not. It depends on the type of comparisons you're making with this data. It's definitely interesting to note that there are clearly multiple ways of coming up with each country's time series. The main point I'm driving home here is that when we choose a low sampling rate, we might miss this point altogether.

Let's consider a different, real-world example of dealing with time-series data that involves attempting to predict a highly volatile economic variable – unemployment.

Pitfall 5D: Funky Forecasts

Each February, the U.S. Bureau of Labor Statistics releases the average unemployment rate (not seasonally adjusted) for the previous year. Historical records are kept, so you can see annual unemployment rates going back to 1947.[3]

Another thing that happens right around this time is that the president's Office of Management and Budget also publishes their forecasts for a number of economic indicators, including unemployment. The forecast covers the current year and another 10 years into the future.

Additionally, the Obama White House preserved and published a record of all of the previously released forecasts going all the way back to President Ford's administration in 1975.[4] The forecasts actually changed from a five-year time horizon to a ten-year time horizon in FY1997 of Bill Clinton's presidency.

What this provides us with, then, is an interesting opportunity to match up what each administration predicted unemployment to be with what it actually turned out to be. In Figure 6.11, the dark line represents the actual average annual unemployment and the thin blue and red lines represent forecasts made by Democratic and Republican presidents, respectively. Thin vertical lines indicate each president's four-year or eight-year time in office.

What does this tell us? It indicates pretty clearly that no matter what the unemployment situation actually was – whether it was on the rise or on the decline – each president's staff predicted a return to around 5% average annual unemployment. Of course, unemployment moves in waves with the economy, so it's just not realistic to predict an almost perfectly steady unemployment rate for a whole decade, as George W. Bush's team did in FY 2008, or as Clinton's team did in FY 1998.

---

[3] https://www.bls.gov/cps/prev_yrs.htm.
[4] https://obamawhitehouse.archives.gov/sites/default/files/omb/budget/fy2017/assets/historicadministrationforecasts.xls.

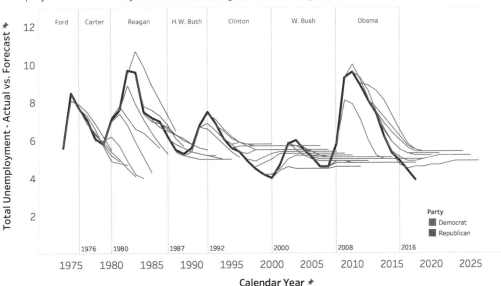

Unemployment forecasts by the Office of Management and Budget of various Whitehouses

FIGURE 6.11 Unemployment forecasts by the Office of Management and Budget of various White House administrations.

Most presidents have done just that, though. They have predicted a fairly immediate return to the 4% to 6% range.

When actual unemployment spiked in 2009, did any of the previous forecasts, including the ones that were published only a year or two prior to the ramp-up, predict the rising trend? Of course not. Can you imagine the uproar it would cause? "In spite of record low unemployment, the president's staff is predicting a rapid increase in unemployment that will begin in two years' time." Here's a highlighted version of the previous chart that shows the actual unemployment, and Bush's glib prediction in FY 2008 (Figure 6.12).

Now you may say, "Ben, there's a big difference between what a politician thinks is going to happen, and what he or she is willing to say to the general public is going to happen." And I'd agree with that. No one is accusing them of being sincere here. But I do think it's interesting that presidents continue to publish this fiction. And I do think it's interesting that an annual prediction of "things are about to return to a sane level" gets any attention whatsoever.

Unemployment forecasts by the Office of Management and Budget of various Whitehouses

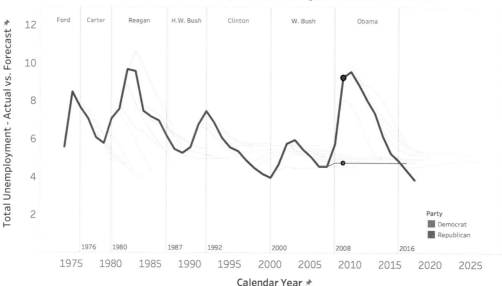

FIGURE 6.12   Unemployment forecasts.

There are honest predictions, and there are things we tell ourselves to make ourselves feel better. I think it's clear which we're dealing with here.

Pitfall 5E: Moronic Measures

It's relatively obvious that life expectancy and unemployment are metrics that matter. They can be confusing and controversial, but tracking how long people live and how many people are out of work is not controversial at all. But that's just not the case for all metrics.

Data is used to measure and compare human beings in many ways in the world we live in. We get accustomed at a very young age through the school system to being tracked, scored, assessed, and ultimately judged by numbers and figures. This typically continues well into our adult lives – sales reps get ranked based on performance to quota, employees get their annual performance review, authors and professors get rated online, and so on.

These numbers and figures can be related to different kinds of things:

- They can be based on our **levels of activity** – how much did we do something?
- They can be the subjective **opinions of others** – what did someone or some group of people think of us?
- They can be some objective **measure of results**, performance, or output – what was the result of our efforts?

High achievers and competitive people can react pretty strongly to news about poor performance scores, no matter what the metric. That fact was on display during the 2018 North American professional basketball league playoffs, when global basketball star LeBron James, playing for the professional team in Cleveland at the time, was told by a sports reporter that he's recording the slowest average speed of anyone on the floor thus far in the Eastern Conference finals series that was being played against the team from Boston.[5] This metric is based on the league's relatively new player tracking system.

Is the Best Player Really the Slowest?

Technically, the reporter was right, at least as much as we trust the accuracy of the player tracking system. It was actually worse than just that series, though. As amazing as he is, James was, in fact, tied with one other player for dead last out of the 60 players who had played 8 or more games with player tracking activated in that year's playoffs.

So what was James's reaction to this information?

> *That's the dumbest sh*t I've ever heard. That tracking bullsh*t can kiss my a**. The slowest guy? Get out of here.*

So, basically, he didn't like it. He didn't stop there:

---

[5] https://theathletic.com/363766/2018/05/22/final-thoughts-on-lebron-james-and-the-speed-required-to-tie-this-series/.

Tell them to track how tired I am after the game, track that sh*t. I'm No. 1 in the NBA on how tired I am after the game.

Thou Dost Protest Too Much

What I find most interesting is that he didn't object along the lines that I thought would be most obvious – to point to his league-leading scoring statistics,[6] his freakishly high efficiency and game impact metrics,[7] or his team's incredible play to that point. Those would be objections about the use of an **activity metric** (how fast was he running up and down the court) instead of an **output metric** (how much was he actually contributing and helping his team to win).

He could have just laughed and said, "Imagine what I could do if I actually ran hard." But no – he took exception to a metric that seemed to indicate he wasn't trying hard. He appealed to something else entirely – how tired he felt after the game – to counteract that implication.

Is Average Speed a Bogus Metric?

So is it the "dumbest sh*t" to use this particular metric to track basketball player performance in the first place? Is average speed over the course of a game a good performance indicator of that player's contribution to the outcome of the game? Perhaps not.

But is there a better way to measure a player's actual impact on a game? It turns out there are many different ways to measure this. An interesting way to measure player contribution is known as PIE – Player Impact Estimate – and it seeks to measure "a player's overall statistical contribution against the total statistics in games in which they play." Or, "in its simplest terms, PIE shows what % of game events did that player or team achieve."[8]

Of course, no one would be surprised to find out that LeBron had the highest PIE of any player in the playoffs at that point, and it

---

[6] https://stats.nba.com/leaders/.
[7] https://stats.nba.com/players/advanced/?sort=PIE&dir=-1&CF=MIN*GE*15&Season=2017-18&SeasonType=Playoffs.
[8] https://stats.nba.com/help/glossary/#pie.

wasn't even close. LeBron was involved in 23.4% of game events by that point in the 2018 playoffs. The next closest player was Victor Oladipo of the Indiana Pacers with a PIE of 19.3.

So how does average speed relate to PIE? If LeBron was last in the former and first in the latter, we'd guess that there's not a strong positive correlation. And we'd guess right. If we correlate average speed with PIE, we see that there's a very weak correlation (the coefficient of determination, R^2, is only 0.056) (Figure 6.13).

What's interesting is that this view shows that LeBron is way up in the top left corner of this chart – he had a low average speed and a high player impact estimate compared to other players. But as it

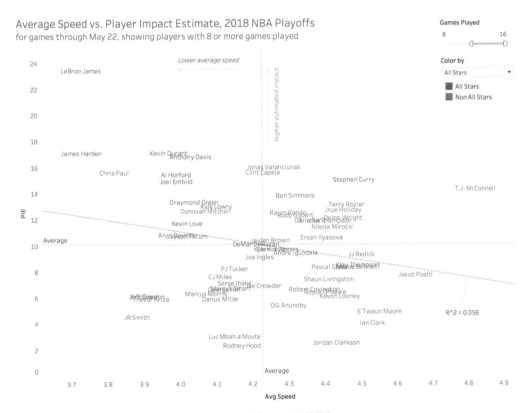

FIGURE 6.13 Average speed versus player impact estimate.

turned out, he was in really good company in this top left quadrant, with 10 of the 12 remaining 2018 All-Stars also in this space. It would appear that the very best players don't seem to have to run fast over the course of an entire game.

It's interesting to compare the lessons from this situation with the way an analyst might present performance scores in a company. The analyst should seek to get buy-in from stakeholders before sharing performance metrics with them. People tend to take measurements of their effort and performance very personally. I know I do. We'd do well to relax a little about that, but it's human nature.

We should also take care to put the emphasis on the metrics that actually matter. If a metric doesn't matter, we shouldn't use it to gauge performance. And activity and opinion metrics are one thing, but they should always be secondary in importance to output or performance scores. Just measuring how much people do something will simply prompt them to increase the volume on that particular activity. Just measuring how much someone else approves of them will lead them to suck up to that person. We all want to contribute to a winning team, and our personal performance metrics should reflect that.

At the same time, though, data is data, and tracking things can help in interesting ways. Perhaps the training staff could use the average speed data to track a player's recovery from an injury. Or perhaps a certain, *ahem*, all-star player later in his career could benefit from keeping average speed down to conserve energy for the final round. Or perhaps a coaching staff could evaluate their team's performance when they play an "up-tempo" style versus running the game at a slower place. Who knows?

In other words, data is only "the dumbest sh*t you've ever heard" when it's used for the wrong things.

Chapter Seven

Pitfall 6: Graphical Gaffes

"Visualization gives you answers to questions you didn't know you had."

—*Ben Schneiderman*

How We Visualize Data

There are two reasons I wanted to write this book in the first place. The first reason is that I noticed students in the data classes I teach were making a lot of the same mistakes on their assignments that I had made when I started my own data journey many years ago. What if there were a book that pointed out a number of these common mistakes to them? Would my students make these errors less often? Would I have made the same mistakes less often if I had read such a book back when I first started?

I'm not just talking about creating bad charts, though. I'm talking about the types of mistakes we've covered thus far – thinking about data and using it inappropriately, getting the stats and calculations wrong, using dirty data without knowing it – you name it.

That leads me to the second reason I wanted to write this book. It seemed to me that a large portion of the conversation about data visualization on social media was centering on which chart type to use and not use, and how to get the visual encodings and channels right.

Poor maligned chart types like the pie chart and the word cloud were getting bullied at every corner of the "dataviz" online play-ground. Everyone who was "in the know" seemed to hate these chart types as well as a few others, like packed bubble charts. Some even declared them to be "evil," and others signaled their membership in the "Dataviz Cool Kidz Club" by ridiculing someone who had just published one.

I don't think there's actually a club with that name, by the way, but you get my point.

Now I'm not saying pie charts, word clouds, or bubble charts are always great choices; there are many situations in which they're not very useful or effective. Even when you *can* make a case that they're warranted, they're quite easy to get wrong. Anyone teaching data to new learners should make that clear.

On the other hand, though, I thought about all the times I made a beautiful bar chart that adhered to all the various gurus' edicts, only to find out later that I had made my sanctioned masterpiece with fundamentally flawed data, or based on wonky calculations that should never have been computed in the first place. Did anyone scoff at these purveyors of pure falsehood? No – they were bar charts, after all.

That's why the first five pitfalls were all dedicated to problems that appear in the process *before* we get around to presenting visuals to an audience. As we've seen, there are many such pitfalls, and they're often hard to spot. These pitfalls don't always get noticed or talked about.

To mix my metaphors, the first five pitfalls are the part of the iceberg that's below the surface.

But of course, the ones that are easier to notice – that is, the highly *visual* ones – do tend to get a lot of ink and press. And well they should. As the part of the process with which our audience directly interacts, the visuals we create matter a great deal. Making mistakes in this crucial part of the process would be like throwing an interception from the 1-yard line at the very end of the American football championship game. We made it *all that way* and put in *all that hard work* to avoid so many other mistakes. What a shame it would be to fail at the very end.

Hopefully, though, I've made the case in the first six chapters of this book that graphical gaffes aren't the *only* potential pitfalls we encounter when working with data. If you agree with me on that point, then I've accomplished one of my main goals already.

So with that out of the way, I'd like to shift my focus in this chapter to the ways we get the pixels wrong when we create abstract visual representations from our data. These pitfalls are, without a doubt, critical to be aware of and avoid.

Pitfall 6A: Challenging Charts

Much has already been written about which charts work well and which don't work so well in different scenarios. There are even beautiful diagrams and posters that arrange chart type icons according to each chart's common purpose, such as to show change over time, or the distribution of a variable, or part-to-whole relationships.

I recommend you take a look at one of the many chart chooser graphics, such as Jon Schwabish's Graphic Continuum[1] or the *Financial Times*'s Visual Vocabulary.[2] These are great for helping you see the realm of the possible, and for considering how charts relate to one another and can be grouped.

---

[1] https://policyviz.com/2014/09/09/graphic-continuum/.
[2] https://github.com/ft-interactive/chart-doctor/tree/master/visual-vocabulary.

I also recommend the book *Creating More Effective Graphs* by Naomi Robbins for a close look at different problems that we can run into when creating charts, or *How Charts Lie* by Alberto Cairo, which effectively lays out various ways we can be misled by charts and chart choices. In these books you will find numerous graphical gaffes to avoid.

On top of these helpful pieces created by talented practitioners, much academic research has been carried out to help us understand how the human mind makes sense of quantitative information encoded in visual form. Tamara Munzner, a well-known and highly respected data visualization researcher at the University of British Columbia, has put together a priceless textbook in *Visualization Analysis & Design*. I've been teaching with this book at the University of Washington's Continuum College for the past few years. It's very thorough and rigorous.

I don't intend to repeat or summarize the contents of these amazing resources in this chapter. Instead, I'd like to relate how people, including and especially myself, can fail in the crucial step of chart selection and creation.

But you definitely won't hear me say, "Chart Type A is good, Chart Type B is bad, and Chart Type C is downright evil." I just don't think about it that way.

To me, chart types are somewhat like letters in the English language. There are "e" and "t" charts (bar charts, line charts), and there are "q" and "z" charts (pie charts, word clouds). The former are used to great effect in many, many cases, and the latter don't find appropriate and effective usage very often at all. Figure 7.1 shows how often the 26 different letters of the English alphabet are used in English text, and I imagine we could make a similar histogram showing effective chart usage frequency.

It's perfectly okay with me that some charts are used more frequently than others. However, I think it makes no sense at all to banish any single chart to oblivion just because it's rarely used or easy to get wrong. Should we get rid of the letter "j" just because

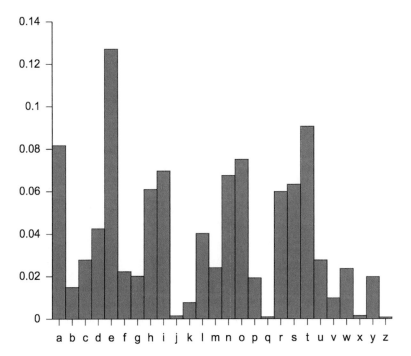

FIGURE 7.1 Relative frequencies of letters in English text.
Source: https://en.wikipedia.org/wiki/Letter_frequency#/media/File:English_letter_
frequency_(alphabetic).svg. Public domain.

it isn't used very often in the English language? I sure hope not, for obvious personal reasons. We'd only be limiting ourselves if we did. This will be a refrain of the current chapter.

But while no one is advocating that we eliminate certain letters from the alphabet – at least no one of whom I'm aware – there definitely are people who are lobbying to get rid of certain chart types altogether.

"Okay, fair enough," you say, "then what *are* the pitfalls we can fall into when we go to choose and build a particular chart to visualize data for an audience?"

Let's look at them.

Instead of taking the typical approach of listing common blunders like truncating a bar chart's y-axis or using 333 slices in a pie chart,

I'm going to break up this category of pitfalls into three subcategories that are based on what I consider to be three distinct *purposes* of data visualizations.

Data visualizations are either used (1) to help people complete a task, or (2) to give them a general awareness of the way things are, or (3) to enable them to explore the topic for themselves. The pitfalls in these three subcategories are quite a bit different.

Data Visualization for Specific Tasks

This first subcategory is by far the most important for businesses. In this scenario, the chart or graph is like a hammer or a screwdriver: a person or group of people is using it to perform a very specific task, to get a job done.

Think about a supply chain professional placing orders with vendors to keep raw materials in stock while minimizing inventory carrying costs. Or think about an investor deciding which assets in a portfolio to buy, sell, and hold on a particular day. Wouldn't they commonly use data visualizations to do these tasks?

In the case of such job aides, designing the tool to fit the exact user or users and the specific details of their task is critical. It's not unlike the process of designing any instrument or application. It's just another type of thing for which the principles of user interface design apply.

Whenever a data visualization is being used primarily as a tool, it's necessary to develop a deep understanding of four key elements in order to identify requirements and how to validate that they have been met:

- **User:** Who is the person or people who will be using it, what do they care about, and why do they care about those things?
- **Task:** What task or tasks do they need to get done, how often, what questions do they need to answer, or what information do they need to gather in order to do it well, both in terms of quality and timeliness?

- **Data:** What data is relevant to the job and what needs to be done to make use of it?
- **Performance:** How does the final deliverable need to behave in order to be useful, such as dimensions and resolution, or data refresh frequency?

Let's consider a simple illustrative scenario in which the chart choice and the way it's built don't exactly help a certain person do a specific task. Instead of dreaming up a fake business scenario and using some fabricated sales database (I really struggle with made-up data), I'll use a personal example just to demonstrate the point.

Every April 30, I hike to the top of Mount Si in North Bend, Washington, just outside of Seattle, where I live. As I've mentioned, I love spending time on the trails and just being around the trees and the views. I know, it's corny, but I feel like it helps me balance out the data-heavy, digital side of my life.

To be fair, though, I do wear a GPS watch and geek out on the trip stats when I get home. So I don't quite manage to leave behind my inner data nerd in the car at the trailhead. That's okay with me for now.

Why April 30? That was the day my father passed away in 2015. When I heard the news, I knew I needed to climb that mountain to clear my mind and just find a way to be with him somehow, some way. Whether he was or wasn't there isn't the point and doesn't really matter to me. He was there in my thoughts.

Wait, how does any of this relate to graphical gaffes or pitfalls or anything? Good question. I'm getting there. Thanks for indulging me.

It's May 3 as I'm writing this right now, and I just finished doing my annual remembrance pilgrimage a few days ago. It happened to be a particularly clear day, and I had a lot of work to get done later that day, so I wanted to start the hike while it was still dark and see if I could get to the top in time to catch the sunrise, which was to take place at 5:54 a.m. Last year when I went to do this hike, I left early in search of the sunrise as well, but there was a huge fog covering the top of the mountain. It was difficult enough to see the trail that morning, much less the horizon.

But last year's trip provided something of value to me for this time around: my trip stats, including a full record of the time, elevation gain, and distance traveled over the course of the trek.

So that's my starting point. Let's go through the four key elements to get our bearings:

1. **User:** Ben Jones, hiker and data geek extraordinaire
   - Cares about having an inspiring sunrise hike to the top of Mount Si
   - Why? To remember his father, get some exercise, and enjoy nature

2. **Task:** Get to the top of Mount Si at or just before sunrise
   - How often? Once per year
   - Answers/information needed?
     i. What time will the sun rise on April 30 in North Bend, Washington?
     ii. How long will it take to get to the top of Mount Si?
     iii. How much buffer time is needed to account for variation in trip time?
   - What does success look like?
     i. Arriving at the of the mountain before sunrise
     ii. Not arriving more than 15 minutes before sunrise, to avoid a long, cold wait

3. **Data:** Sunrise info from search query, detailed Mount Si hiking stats from previous trek
   - Sunrise time is a single constant; no data prep needed
   - Historical trek stats can be obtained from watch app and/or fitness social network
   - Buffer time is a choice based on assumed variability in travel time

4. **Performance:** No data refresh needed; analysis based on static data only

I'll keep it simple and leave out of this example the time it takes me to drive from my house to the trailhead as well as the time it'll take me to get out of bed, fully dressed, and on the road. Those are the other pieces of information I'll need to set my alarm before going to bed. But for the purposes of this example, we'll stick with hike start time as our task and objective.

At this point, all I need from the visuals of my previous trip is a good idea of how long it will take me to get to the top of the mountain, which I can deduct, along with a 15-minute buffer, from the 5:54 a.m. sunrise time to determine the time I'll need to start on the trail.

A quick download of my data allowed me to recreate what I saw when I went to my online fitness portal, more or less (Figure 7.2).

Ben's April 30th, 2018 hike to the top of Mount Si

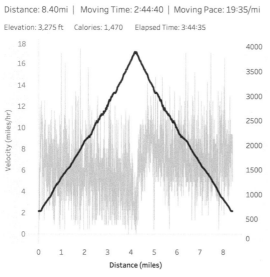
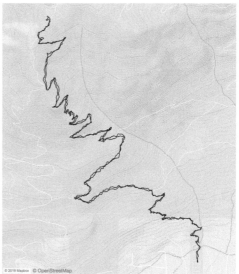

FIGURE 7.2 A recreation of the data visualizations my fitness network site provided.

As I looked at these charts, I realized that they didn't really allow me to get a good answer to my question. The dashboard gave me many helpful pieces of information – the total round-trip distance, the total time I was moving, as well as the total elapsed time (minus stationary resting time), and an elevation profile as a function of distance travelled. I knew I went up and came straight back, so I assumed that the trail to the top was close to 4 miles long, and I could see that I was moving at a pace of around 20 minutes per mile over the course of the entire trip. But I could also see that my pace was faster on the way down from the top, so I couldn't really rely on this variable to do some back-of-the-napkin math to determine the time to the top based on distance and velocity. Not at the level of precision I was looking for, anyway. There was too much of a chance I'd miss the 15-minute window of time I was shooting for between 5:39 a.m. and 5:54 a.m.

Now, this isn't intended to be a criticism of the fitness social network where I store my trip stats. While I was genuinely surprised that I didn't find a single chart with time on the horizontal x-axis, I'd have to acknowledge that they didn't exactly set out to design this dashboard for my specific task of determining when to start on the trail to catch a glimpse of the sunrise that morning.

That being said, I was able to download my stats and do a quick dashboard redesign in Tableau to better suit my needs. Doing so allowed me to see very quickly that I reached the top of the mountain almost exactly two hours after I left my car at the trailhead the previous year (Figure 7.3).

Notice that I added two new charts with time on the horizontal axis. The first shows a timeline of my altitude in the top left corner. The second shows a timeline of total distance traveled in the bottom left corner. The altitude timeline is most helpful in my specific scenario because it's immediately obvious how long it took me to get to the top – the x-value corresponding to beginning of the middle plateau of the curve – 2 hours.

On other hikes, however, there may be no mountain to climb. The path could just be a loop around a lake, or an "out-and-back" along

Ben's April 30th, 2018 hike to the top of Mount Si

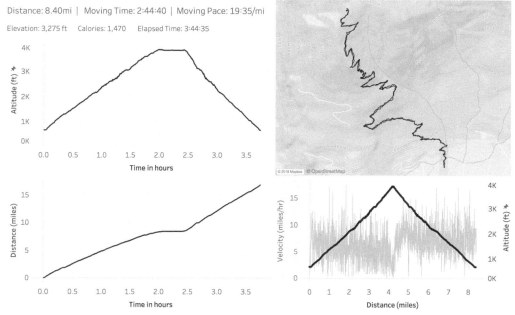

Distance: 8.40mi | Moving Time: 2:44:40 | Moving Pace: 19:35/mi

Elevation: 3,275 ft   Calories: 1,470   Elapsed Time: 3:44:35

FIGURE 7.3   My extended analysis of my 2018 trip stats.

the shore of a river. In such cases, altitude might not be as helpful to determine the time it would take to reach a certain point along the path between the start and the finish. For those cases, time on the x-axis and distance traveled on the y-axis – the bottom left chart – will enable me find to the amount of time it took to reach any point along the path.

This time-distance view also helps because it lets me visually identify any long periods of rest – horizontal portions of the line where time keeps going but distance doesn't. Maybe I stopped to read a book, or eat lunch, or take some photographs. In this instance, I can see clearly that the only time I really stopped moving was for about 30 minutes right after reaching the top of the mountain. I can't use horizontal sections of the time-altitude view for this same purpose because it's possible that a horizontal section of this line corresponds with a flat section of the trail where I was still moving but at a constant elevation.

So now I have the final variable for my equation – estimated ascent time – and I was able to complete my simple task to determine the time to leave my car at the trailhead in order to make it to the top in time for sunrise:

$$\text{5:54 a.m. sunrise time} - \text{2 hr ascent time} - \text{15 min buffer} = \text{3:39 a.m. trip start time}$$

And how'd the sunrise hike go, after all that? Well, I slept through my alarm and didn't start on the trail until 8:00 a.m. So it goes. Next year, for sure.

Now this may seem like a strange approach to begin to describe graphical gaffes. In many ways, it wasn't even a gaffe at all. The social network designed their dashboard; it didn't happen to help me do a rather specific task. There's no horrendous pie chart with 333 slices, no ghastly packed bubble chart. Just a line chart and a map that didn't help me complete my task.

Notice I didn't go into detail about whether line charts or bar charts are the "right" choice in this instance, or whether a dual axis for the altitude and velocity line chart was kosher or not. I think those debates can tend to miss the point. In this case, what was needed was a line chart, but one with time as the x-axis rather than distance in miles. The problem wasn't the chart type. It was the choice of the variable mapped to one of the axes.

My goal in using this example is to illustrate that "good enough" is highly dependent on the details of the task our audience needs to perform. It would be easy to start listing off various rules of thumb to use when choosing charts. Others have certainly done that to great effect. But if you're building something for someone who needs to perform a certain task or tasks, the final product will have to stand the test of usage. Pointing to a data viz guru's checklist will not save you if your users can't get their job done.

Data Visualization for General Awareness

Some visualizations aren't built in order to help someone perform a specific task or function. These types of visualizations lack a direct and immediate linkage to a job, unlike the ones we just considered.

Think about the times you've seen a chart on a news site showing the latest unemployment figures, or a slide in a presentation by an executive in your company that shows recent sales performance. Many times you aren't being asked to take facts in those charts and use them to perform any specific action right then and there, or even in the near future, or at all. Other people might be using these same exact visuals in that way – as tools – but some people who see them don't need to carry out a function other than just to become aware, to update their understanding of the way things are or have been.

As presenters of data visualizations, often we just want our audience to understand something about their environment – a trend, a pattern, a breakdown, a way in which things have been progressing. If we ask ourselves what we want our audience to *do* with that information, we might have a hard time coming up with a clear answer sometimes. We might just want them to *know* something.

What pitfalls can we fall into when we seek to simply *inform* people using data visualizations – nothing more, nothing less? Let's take a look at a number of different types of charts that illustrate these pitfalls. We'll stick with a specific data set to do so: reported cases of crime in Orlando, Florida.[3] I visited Orlando in 2018 to speak and train at a journalism conference, and I found this data set so that my audience could learn using data that was relevant to our immediate surroundings.

---

[3] https://data.cityoforlando.net/Orlando-Police/OPD-Crimes/4y9m-jbmz.

The data set on the city of Orlando's open data portal comes with the following description:

> This dataset comes from the Orlando Police Department records management system. It includes all Part 1 and Part 2 crimes as defined by the FBI's Uniform Crime Reporting standards. When multiple crimes are committed the highest level of crime is what is shown. The data includes only Open and Closed cases and does not include informational cases without arrests. This data excludes crimes where the victim or offender data is or could be legally protected.

This paragraph is followed by a long list of excluded crimes, including domestic violence, elderly abuse, and a list of sexual offenses, among others. So it's important to note that this data set says nothing about those types of crimes.

It's also important to note, going back to our discussion about the gap between data and reality in our chapter on epistemic errors, that we're not looking at *actual* crime, just *reported* crime. There's a difference. The site where I found the data also includes a disclaimer that "operations and policy regarding reporting might change," so be careful about considering comparisons over time. In other words, a jump or a dip in one type of reported crime could be due to a change in the way police are doing their jobs, not necessarily due to a change in criminal activity itself. Not mentioning these caveats and disclaimers is misleading in and of itself. It can be inconvenient for us to do so because we might feel it will pull the rug out from under our own feet as we seek to make a powerful case to our audience. But it's just not ethical to omit these details once we know them.

1. Showing them a chart that's misleading
If we wanted to impress upon our audience that reported cases of narcotics are on the rise in Orlando, chances are that if we show them this 40-week timeline, we'd affect their understanding quite convincingly (Figure 7.4).

Rising Narcotics Cases in Orlando

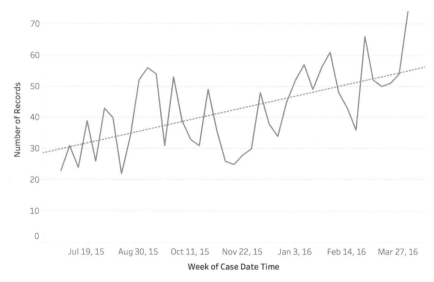

FIGURE 7.4 Reported cases of narcotics crimes in Orlando for 41 weeks, June 2015–April 2016.

There's nothing factually incorrect about this chart at all. It's not even poorly designed. But it's terribly misleading. Why?

Because if we open up the time window on the horizontal axis and explore the trend of reported cases of narcotics covering the entire 8-year period, the data tells a very different story. The initial 40-week period is shown in the shaded gray region in Figure 7.5.

Now, this may be an innocent case of failing to examine the trend in broader context. Or it may be a case of outright deception by intentional cherry-picking. In either case, though, we have made a tremendous graphical gaffe by showing our audience something that left them with the exact wrong impression.

It's possible to play with the configurations of many different types of charts to mislead an audience. This is just one simple example. I'll refer you once again to Alberto Cairo's *How Charts Lie*, as well as an older book by Darrell Huff, *How to Lie with Statistics*.

Declining Narcotics Cases in Orlando

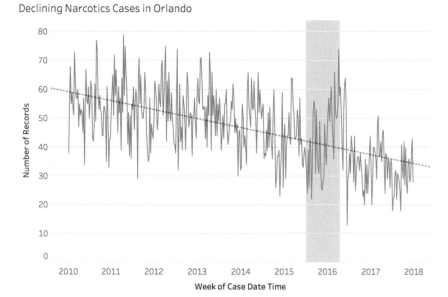

FIGURE 7.5   Weekly reported cases of narcotics crimes in Orlando, 2010–2017.

The fact that it's possible to pull the wool over people's eyes in this way has caused many to be wary of statistics for a very long time. The following quote comes from a book called *Chartography in Ten Lessons*[4] by Frank Julian Warne that was published in 1919, a full century prior to the year in which I am finishing writing this book:

> To the average citizen statistics are as incomprehensible as a Chinese puzzle. To him they are a mental "Mystic Moorish Maze." He looks upon columns of figures with suspicion because he cannot understand them. Perhaps he has so often been misled by the wrong use of statistics or by the use of incorrect statistics that he has become skeptical of them as representing reliable evidence as to facts and, like an automaton, he mechanically repeats "while figures may not lie, all liars, figure," or the equally common libel, "there are three kinds of lies – lies, damn lies and statistics."

---

[4] https://play.google.com/books/reader?id=8SQoAAAAYAAJ&printsec=-frontcover&pg=GBS.PR3.

Misleading people with charts injects some bad karma into the universe. We're still paying for the decisions of a few generations ago that led people into this exact pitfall. As a result, the collective human psyche is quite wary that data and charts are likely purveyors of trickery and falsehood, not truth.

2. Showing them a chart that's confusing

Slightly less egregious than the previous type of chart that misleads is the one that confuses an audience. The only reason this type of pitfall isn't as bad is because our audience doesn't walk away with the *wrong* idea. They walk away with *no idea at all*, just a bewildering feeling that they must've missed something.

There are really many more ways to confuse people with data than I can list or explain here. Many basic charts are confusing to people, let alone more complex ones such as a box-and-whisker plot. Does this mean we stop using them? No, but we may need to take a moment to orient our audience so that they understand what they're looking at.

But one of the most common ways to confuse someone with a chart is to include too much in the view. For example, if we wanted to focus our audience's attention on reported cases of shoplifting, and we showed them this timeline, we'd be right at the bottom of this pitfall (Figure 7.6).

Do you see what happens when you look at this chart? If you're like me, you make an honest and even an earnest attempt to verify that the presenter or the writer of the accompanying text is telling you something accurate. You struggle to find what you're looking for, and you start to get confused and then frustrated. The lines and the colors and the way they cross and overlap just make your brain scream when it can't find the information it's looking for. And then you give up.

Why do we insist on showing so much data to our audience all the time? It's like there's this irresistible temptation to include everything in the view, as if we'll get extra credit for adding all that data

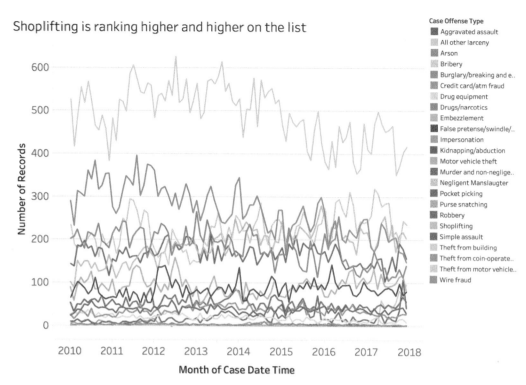

FIGURE 7.6   A line chart showing 24 different categories of reported crimes in Orlando.

we've played with. Are we trying to impress them? We're not, we're just confusing them. Strip away all the extraneous stuff, or at least let it fade into the background.

You might hear this type of chart referred to as a "spaghetti chart" for obvious reasons. Notice a few things about it, if you don't mind. First, notice that "Shoplifting" has been given a light beige color. This was assigned as a default from the Tableau Desktop product I used to create it. Now, there's nothing inherently wrong with beige, but it sure is hard to pick the beige line out of the jumbled lines. If that happens to be the default assignment for the exact line or mark to which we want to draw attention, we will want to change it to something more noticeable.

Next, consider how many different lines there are. If you count the items in the legend, you'll see that there are 24 different lines. But there are only 20 different colors in the default color palette that the software applied to the offense type variable. So when it gets to the 21st item in the alphabetically ordered list, the software applies the same color that it applied to the first item. The 22nd item gets the same color as item number 2, and so on. Accepting defaults like that can be a rookie mistake, to be sure, but I've made that mistake many times, and many times well after I've been able to call myself a rookie.

What's the effect of this color confounding (which we'll consider more in the next chapter)? Take a look at the top line. It's light blue. Find light blue in the legend. To what offense type does it correspond? Does it correspond to "All other larceny" or "Theft from building"? We can't tell just by looking at the static version. We'd need to hover over an interactive version, or click on the legend to see that it's the "All other larceny" category. If a chart requires interaction to answer an important question, but it's presented in static form, then that's a surefire way to confuse people.

Going back to our original goal of bringing awareness to the shoplifting data, we can change the color for "Shoplifting" from light beige to something bolder, a color that's uniquely assigned to that value. Then, since our point is about the increase in rank, we'll leave the other lines in the view instead of removing them altogether, but we'll give them a lighter appearance or apply transparency to them to make the line series we want our audience to notice stand out (Figure 7.7).

Taking the time to make these minor but important tweaks to our charts will go a long way to ensuring our audience isn't staring at the screen or the page with that furrowed brow and that feeling of being completely lost. We don't want that.

3. Showing them a chart that doesn't convey the insight we want to impart
Let's say you and I are trying to educate a group of citizens about the state of reported crimes in Orlando, and we have a slide in which we'd like to make it immediately clear that three categories – theft,

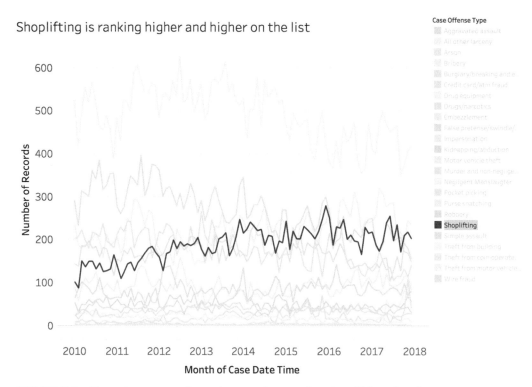

Shoplifting is ranking higher and higher on the list

Case Offense Type
- Aggravated assault
- All other larceny
- Arson
- Bribery
- Burglary/breaking and e...
- Credit card/atm fraud
- Drug equipment
- Drugs/narcotics
- Embezzlement
- False pretense/swindle/...
- Impersonation
- Kidnapping/abduction
- Motor vehicle theft
- Murder and non-neglige...
- Negligent Manslaughter
- Pocket picking
- Purse snatching
- Robbery
- **Shoplifting**
- Simple assault
- Theft from building
- Theft from coin-operate...
- Theft from motor vehicle...
- Wire fraud

Number of Records

Month of Case Date Time

FIGURE 7.7   Focusing our audience's attention on the shoplifting timeline.

burglary, and assault – together have accounted for three out of every four reported crimes. Which of the following four alternatives in Figure 7.8 would you choose to make this point to your audience?

I'd argue that the pie chart and the treemap both make this point fairly well, and that the bar chart and the packed bubble chart don't. The reason is that the pie chart and the treemap each group all of the marks – slices in the case of the pie chart and rectangles in the case of the treemap – into a single, cohesive unit. In the case of the pie chart, the three slices we're asking our audience to pay attention to stop at almost exactly 9 o'clock, or 75% of a whole circle.

I'd argue that using 12 distinct color hues to make a point like this is a bit distracting, and that a simplified version of the color palette would make the point even easier for our audience to observe (Figure 7.9).

Pick the Best Chart: *"Theft, Burglary & Assault accounted for 3/4ths of reported crimes in Orlando between 2010 and 2017."*

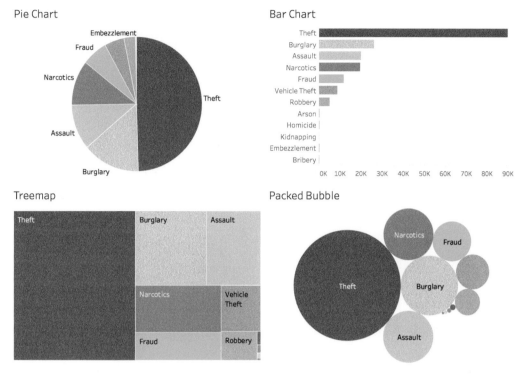

FIGURE 7.8   Four chart types that show number of reported crimes by category.

Notice how the simplified color scheme doesn't really make the share figure any clearer in the case of the bar chart and the packed bubble charts. That's because each mark in these two charts – rectangles in the case of the bar chart and circles in the case of the packed bubble chart – are separated in a way that doesn't give the notion of a cohesive single unit like the others do.

So we have two chart types that make the point we're trying to make abundantly clear and immediately noticeable. But we should ask ourselves another very important question: Is it actually fair and accurate to show this group of reported crimes as a single, whole unit? Think back to the caveats that were listed about this data: it only includes Part 1 and Part 2 crimes based on the FBI's standards.

Pick the Best Chart: *"Theft, Burglary & Assault accounted for 3/4ths of reported crimes in Orlando between 2010 and 2017."*

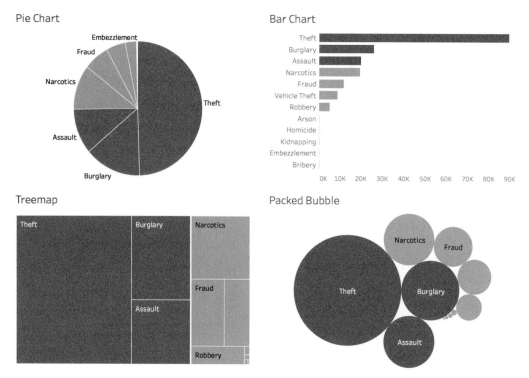

FIGURE 7.9   A simplified color palette to focus on the top three categories.

It only includes cases that were both opened and closed. In the case of multiple crimes, it only includes the highest level. And it doesn't include crimes where the victim or offender's identity could be legally protected.

That's a lot of caveats, isn't it? Does this data set represent a single *anything*, then? Perhaps not. If not, maybe it would be better to use a chart type, like a bar chart, that *doesn't* impart the notion of part-to-whole. If we do decide to show our audience a part-to-whole chart type like a pie chart or a treemap, and certain substantial elements aren't included in the data for whatever reason, we'll want to make that very clear to our audience. If we don't, we can be pretty sure that we'll be misleading them.

*4. Showing them a chart that doesn't convey the insight with
enough precision*

Let's say we wanted to make a different point altogether – that there
have been a similar number of reported cases of assault and narcotics crimes in Orlando from 2010 to 2017, but that cases of assault
have just barely outpaced narcotics over that time period.

Of the following seven charts in Figure 7.10, which would be the
best to accompany this point in a presentation we would deliver or
an article we would write?

Only the bar chart makes this point clear. It's the only one of the
seven where the marks for assault and narcotics share a common
baseline, allowing us to compare their relative count (bar length)
with any degree of precision. With the other six charts, there's really
no way to tell which one of the two categories occurred more often.
It's pretty clear that they're quite close in occurrence, but without
making inferences based on the sort order, there's just no way to tell
without adding labels.

If, for some reason, our audience needs to understand the relative
sizes with even greater precision than the bar chart affords, we can
always add the raw counts and percentages (Figure 7.11).

Adding data values as labels like this is an effective way to enable our
audience to make precise comparisons. A list or table of values alone
would also convey this precision, but it would lack the visual encoding
that conveys patterns and general notions of relative size at a glance.

5. Showing them a chart that misses the real point

In describing this pitfall so far, we have concerned ourselves with
individual charts, and whether they convey our message well to
our audience and provide them with a general awareness that sufficiently matches reality. We have considered ways to create charts
that introduce flaws that mislead, confuse, or provide inadequate
visual corroboration for the point we're trying to make. We can classify these blunders as "sins of commission" – that is, they all involve
an action that produces the problem.

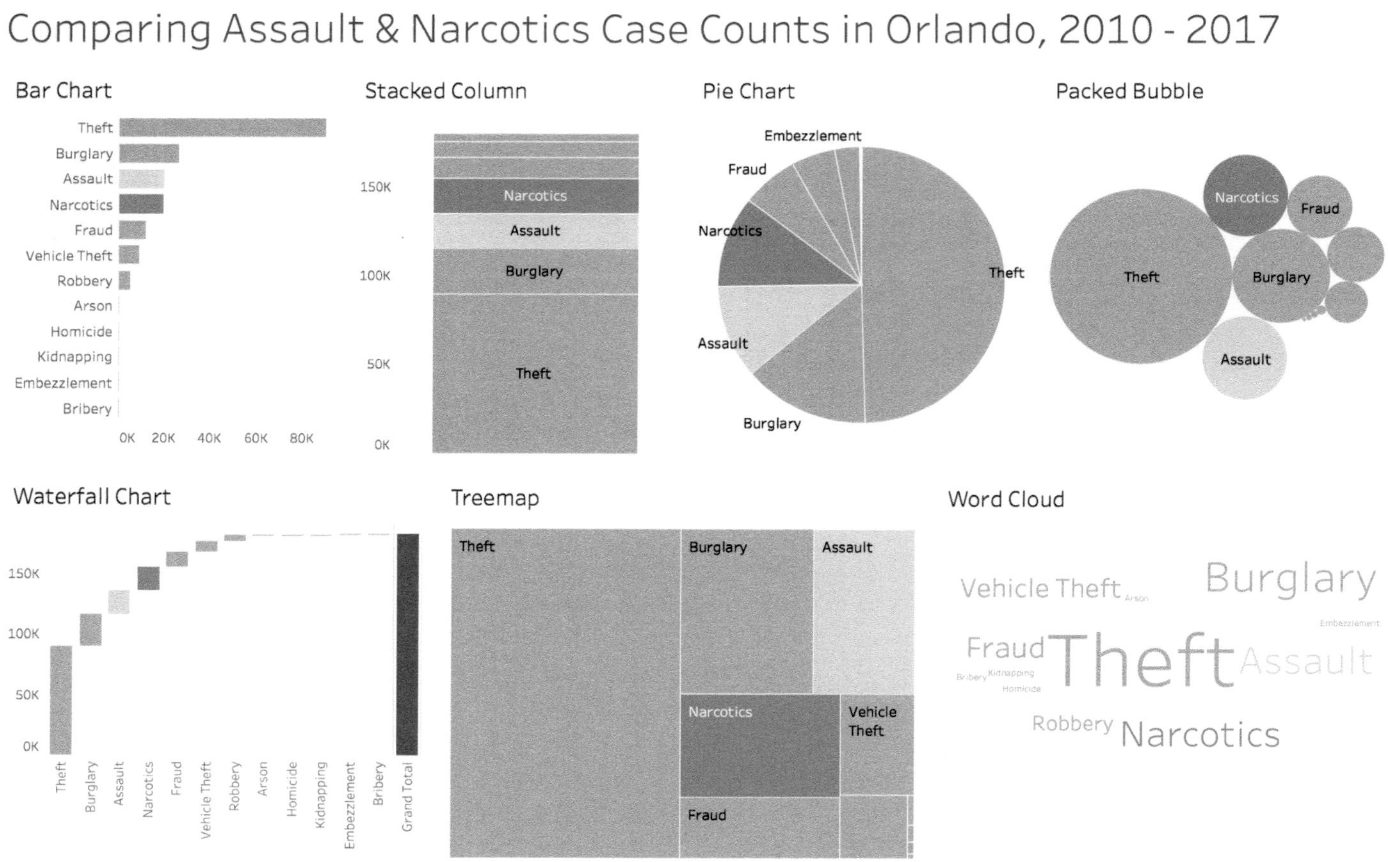

Comparing Assault & Narcotics Case Counts in Orlando, 2010 - 2017

FIGURE 7.10 Seven ways to compare reported cases of assault and narcotics crimes in Orlando.

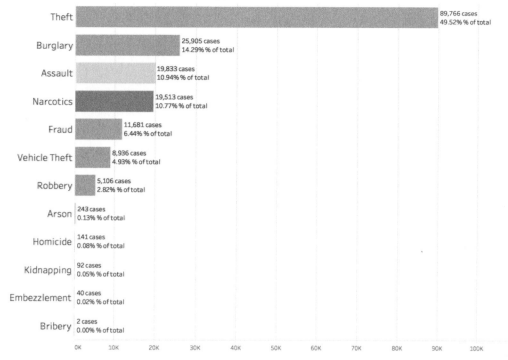

FIGURE 7.11   Adding data labels and gridlines to afford greater precision of comparison.

But there's another way a chart can fail to convey our message. It can miss the point. Like failing to add an exclamation mark to a crucial sentence, or like criticizing the crew of the *Titanic* for their arrangement of the deck chairs, we can leave out something even more important and thereby commit a "sin of omission."

For example, if we wanted to impress upon our audience that theft is the most frequently reported category of Part 1 and Part 2 crimes in Orlando, we could show them the pie chart or treemap in Figure 7.12 to drive home the point that theft accounted for almost half of all such cases between 2010 and 2017.

And if we stopped there, we'd have missed the point. Why? Because if we look at the way the number of reported cases of theft in Orlando has changed on a monthly basis over this time, we'd see that it's growing in overall share (Figure 7.13).

Monthly Reported Crime in Orlando, 2010 - 2017

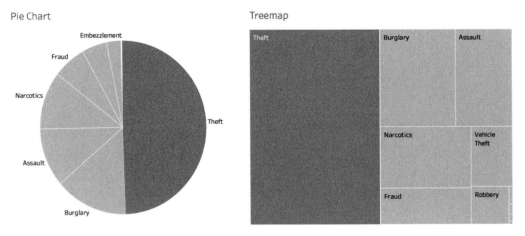

FIGURE 7.12   A pie chart and a treemap that convey that theft accounts for half of the crime.

In fact, if we look at the mix of reported Part 1 and Part 2 crimes in Orlando for 2017 alone, we see that theft accounted for just over 55% of such crimes (Figure 7.14).

Monthly Reported Crime in Orlando, 2010 - 2017

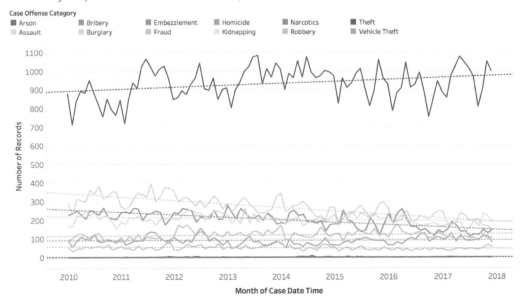

FIGURE 7.13   A timeline showing the change in number of reported cases of crime by category.

Monthly Reported Crime in Orlando, 2017

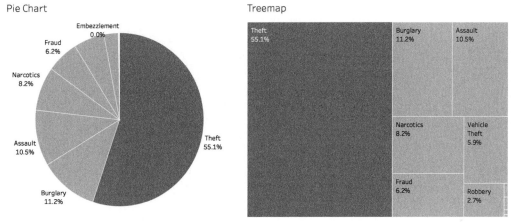

FIGURE 7.14   Breakdown of reported crime by category for 2017.

By comparison, theft accounted for only 45% in 2010 (Figure 7.15).

The bottom line is that we didn't make the point as strongly as we could have. Our original chart selection failed to convey the fact that theft has significantly increased in share over the time period we were showing and is now much higher than it once was.

Monthly Reported Crime in Orlando, 2010

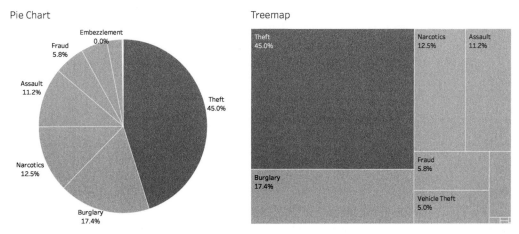

FIGURE 7.15   Breakdown of reported crime by category for 2010.

When we showed the original chart covering 2010 through 2017, did we give our audience a general awareness of reality? Yes, but we didn't make them aware of a fact that's perhaps even more important. We picked the right chart type (assuming we believe we're dealing with a reasonable "whole"), we chose color in such a way as to draw attention to our main point and category of emphasis, and we even added labels for added precision. And we did so with great courage, feeling confident that our pie chart was good enough in spite of the many pie-chart-hating hecklers we knew would throw tomatoes.

But we sold ourselves short by omitting a critical fact.

Data Visualization for Open Exploration

Many times when we create charts, graphs, maps, and dashboards, we do so for our own understanding rather than to present to an audience. We're not in "data storytelling mode" quite yet, we're still in "data story finding mode." That's okay, and there's a time for this critical step in the process. It's actually a very enjoyable step when you enter a state of playful flow with a data set or even multiple data sets. You're deep in the data, finding out interesting things and coming up with brand new questions you didn't know you had, just like the epigraph of this chapter indicates is possible.

I love the way EDA – Exploratory Data Analysis – embraces the messiness and fluid nature of this process. The way we explore data today, we often aren't constrained by rigid hypothesis testing or statistical rigor that can slow down the process to a crawl.

But we need to be careful with this rapid pace of exploration, too. Modern business intelligence and analytics tools allow us to do so much with data so quickly that it can be easy to fall into a pitfall by creating a chart that misleads us in the early stages of the process.

Like a teenager scrolling through an Instagram feed at lightning speed, we fly through a series of charts, but we never actually stop to pay close, diligent attention to any one view. We never actually spend quality time with the data; we just explore in such a rush and then publish or present without ever having slowed down to really see things with clarity and focus.

For example, let's think about that rising trend of reported thefts in Orlando. It was really easy to drag a trendline on top of the line chart and see the line sloping upward and take away from a step that took all of 10 seconds that theft is getting higher and higher each month that goes by. After all, the line is angling upward, right?

But if we consider an individuals control chart[5] (Figure 7.16), which is designed to help us understand whether changes in a time series can be interpreted as signals or mere noise, then we see a slightly different story.

Control Chart Examining Statistical Signals in Reported Theft in Orlando

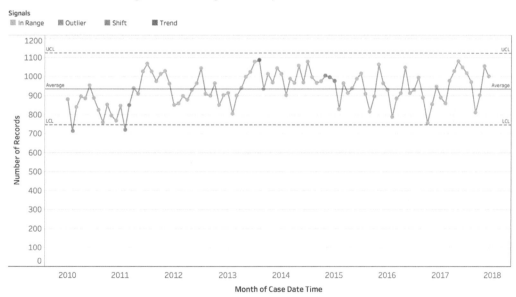

FIGURE 7.16 An individuals control chart showing signals in the time series of reported thefts.

---

[5] https://en.wikipedia.org/wiki/Control_chart.

Yes, there were months in 2010 and 2011 that were lower than we would expect ("outliers" either above the upper control limit – UCL, or below the lower control limit – LCL), and there was even a rising trend in 2013 (6 points or more all increasing or decreasing) and a shift to end 2014 and begin 2015 (9 points or more all on one side of the average line). But since January 2015, the number of reported cases of theft in Orlando hasn't see any statistically significant changes at all. That's 35 straight months of noise. Would a core message that theft is rising and rising every month really be warranted by the data?

If we had just rushed on to the next chart without stopping to look more closely at this one finding, we might have missed the deeper understanding we gained by slowing down and analyzing more deeply.

Pitfall 6B: Data Dogmatism

Like in other forms of expression and communication, there are no black-and-white rules in data visualization, only rules of thumb.

I don't believe that we can ever declare that a particular visualization type either "works" or "doesn't work" in all conceivable instances. This binary approach is very tempting, I'll admit. We get to feel confident that we're avoiding some huge mistake, and we get to feel better about ourselves when we see someone else breaking that particular rule. I started off in this field with that mindset.

The more I've seen and experienced, though, the more I prefer a sliding grayscale of effectiveness over the black-and-white "works"/"doesn't work" paradigm. It's true that some chart choices work better than others, but it's highly dependent on the objective, the audience, and the context.

This paradigm makes it harder to decide what to do and what not to do, but I believe this approach embraces the complexity inherent in the task of communicating with other hearts and minds.

Sometimes the most effective choice in a particular situation might surprise us. Let's consider two fields that are seemingly unrelated to data visualization: chess and writing. Data visualization is like chess in that both involve a huge number of alternative "moves." These moves are subject to common thinking about what gives a player an advantage over their opponent.

For those not familiar with the basics of chess strategy, the different pieces of the board are assigned different points, from the single point of the lowly pawn to the full nine points of the ultra-powerful queen. Generally speaking, a player would not want to lose a queen in exchange for a pawn or other lesser piece. But Russian chess grandmaster Garry Kasparov decided to sacrifice his queen early in a game against Vladimir Kramnik in 1994.[6] He went on to win that game in decisive fashion.

What matters is not who ends up with the most points from pieces on the board, but who puts his opponent's king in checkmate. It's possible, but not exactly common, to achieve checkmate while making some surprising decisions that seem to put the player at a disadvantage, at least in terms of material.

In the second analogy, data visualization is like writing in that both involve communicating complex thoughts and emotions to an audience. Typically, when writing for a reader or group of readers, common rules of spelling, syntax, and grammar apply. Students who break these rules in school get poor grades on their writing. But American novelist, playwright, and screenwriter Cormac McCarthy decided to eschew virtually all punctuation in his 2006 novel *The Road*. He won the 2007 Pulitzer Prize for Fiction for that novel.[7]

Now, would I recommend either of those decisions to a novice chess player or writer? No, but I wouldn't completely eliminate them from the set of all possible solutions, either. A brilliant diagram in Tamara Munzner's *Visualization Analysis & Design* illustrates why (Figure 7.17).

---

[6] https://www.youtube.com/watch?v=VommuOQablw.
[7] https://en.wikipedia.org/wiki/The_Road.

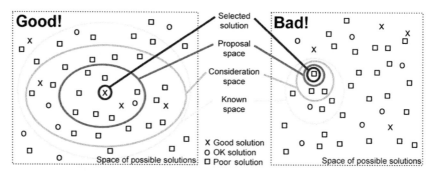

FIGURE 7.17 Two approaches to choosing selecting solutions.

If we start with a larger consideration space shown in the diagram on the left, it's more likely to contain a good solution by virtue of its expansiveness. On the other hand, labeling certain visualization types as "bad" and eliminating them from the set of possible solutions paints us into a corner, as shown in the diagram on the right.

Why do that? Telling a budding chess player *never* to sacrifice a queen, or telling a novice novelist *never* to leave out a period or comma under any circumstances isn't doing them any favors. These decisions can sometimes be made to great effect.

For example, consider the word cloud. Most would argue that it's not terribly useful. Some have even argued that it's downright harmful.[8] There's a good reason for that, and in certain situations it's very true – it will do nothing but confuse your audience.

It's difficult to make precise comparisons using this chart type, without a doubt. Words or sequences with more characters are given more pixels than shorter strings that appear more frequently in the text. And using a word cloud to analyze or describe blocks of text, such as a political debate, is often misleading because the words are considered entirely out of context.

Fair enough. Let's banish all word clouds, then, and malign any software product that makes it possible to create one, right?

---

[8] https://www.niemanlab.org/2011/10/word-clouds-considered-harmful/.

I wouldn't go so far. Word clouds have a valid use, even if it is rare. What if we had a few brief moments during a presentation to impress upon a large room of people, including some sitting way in the back, that there are only a handful of most commonly used passwords, and they're pretty ridiculous. Isn't it at least possible that a word cloud could suffice for this purpose?

Would you choose a bar chart, a treemap, or a packed bubble over a word cloud, in this scenario? You decide (Figure 7.18).

I admit it – I'd likely choose the word cloud in the scenario I described. The passwords jump right off the screen at my audience, even for the folks in the back. It doesn't matter to me whether they can tell that "password" is used 1.23 times more frequently than "123456." That level of precision isn't required for the task I need them to carry out in this hypothetical scenario. The other chart types

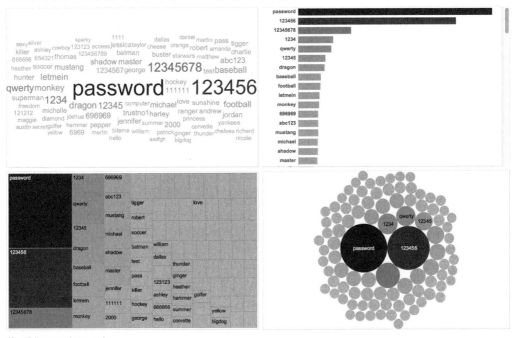

FIGURE 7.18 Four ways to show the 100 most common passwords.

all suffer from the fact that only a fraction of the words even fit in the view at all. The bar chart only has 17 of the top 100 showing, with a vertical scrollbar to access all the others. The packed bubble only lets my audience see five of the passwords before the sequences don't fit in the circles anymore.

With these other three charts, the audience can't scan the full list at a glance to get a general sense of what's contained in it – names, numbers, sports, "batman."

If what you take from this example is that I think word clouds are awesome and you should use them all the time, you've completely missed my meaning. In most instances, word clouds aren't very good at all, just like sacrificing one's queen or omitting quotation marks entirely from a novel.

But every now and then, they do the trick.

Without a doubt, we can list many other scenarios where we would choose one of the other three chart types instead of the word cloud. Choosing a particular chart type depends on many factors. That's a good thing, and frankly, I love that about data visualization.

Since there are so many variables in play, and since we hardly ever know the objective, the audience, or the full context of a particular project, we need to be humble when providing a critique of someone else's data visualization. All we see is a single snapshot of the visual. Was this created as part of a larger presentation or write-up? Did it also include a verbal component when delivered? What knowledge, skills, and attitudes did the intended audience members possess? What are the tasks that needed to be carried out associated with the visualization? What level of precision was necessary to carry out those tasks?

These questions, and many more, really matter. If you're the kind of person who scoffs at the very mention of word clouds, your critique of my example above would be swift and harsh. And it would largely be misguided.

I enjoy that there are so many creative and talented people in the data visualization space who are trying new things. Freedom to innovate is necessary for any field to thrive. But making blanket statements about certain visualization types isn't helpful, and it tends to reduce the overall spirit of freedom to innovate.

"Innovation" doesn't just involve creating new chart types. It can also include using existing chart types in new and creative ways. Or applying current techniques to new and interesting data sets. Or combining data visualization with other forms of expression, visual or otherwise. As long as we can have a respectful and considerate dialogue about what works well and what could be done to improve on the innovation, I say bring it on.

Adding the winning ideas to the known solution space is good for us all.

Pitfall 6C: The Optimize/Satisfice False Dichotomy

In data visualization, is there a single "best" way to visualize data in a particular scenario and for a particular audience, or are there multiple "good enough" ways? This debate has surfaced at least a handful of times in the data visualization world.

Some say there is definitely a best solution in a given situation. Others say it's possible that multiple visuals all suffice in a given situation.

Could both be right?

This is going to sound strange, but I think both are right, and there's room for both approaches in the field of data visualization. Let me explain.

Luckily for us, very intelligent people have been studying how to choose between a variety of alternatives for over a century now. Decision making of this sort is the realm of operations research (also called "operational research," "management science," and "decision science"). Another way of asking the lead-in question is:

> Q: When choosing how to show data to a particular audience, should I keep looking until I find a single optimum solution, or should I stop as soon as I find one of many that achieves some minimum level of acceptability (also called the "acceptability threshold" or "aspiration level")?

The former approach is called optimization, and the latter was given the name "satisficing" (a combination of the words satisfy and suffice) by Nobel laureate Herbert A. Simon in 1956.[9]

So which approach should we take? Should we optimize or satisfice when visualizing data? Which approach we take depends on three factors:

1. Whether or not the decision problem is *tractable*

2. Whether or not all of the information is *available*

3. Whether or not we have *time and resources* to get the necessary information

But what is the "payoff function" for data visualizations?

This is a critical question, and from where I think some of the debate stems. Part of the challenge in ranking alternative solutions to a data visualization problem is determining what variables go into the payoff function, and their relative weight or importance. The payoff function is how we compare alternatives. Which choice is better? Why is it better? How much better?

A few data visualization purists whose work I've read would claim that we can judge the merits of a data visualization by one criterion and one criterion only: namely, whether it makes the data as easy to interpret as possible. By stating this, the purist is proposing a particular payoff function: increased comprehensibility = increased payoff.

---

[9] https://en.wikipedia.org/wiki/Satisficing.

But is comprehensibility the only variable that matters (*did our audience accurately and precisely understand the relative proportions?*) or should other variables be factored in as well, such as:

- Attention (Did our audience take notice?)
- Impact (Did they care about what we showed them?)
- Aesthetics (Did they find the visuals appealing?)
- Memorability (Did they remember the medium and/or the message some time into the future?)
- Behavior (Did they take some desired action as a result?)

Figure 7.19 shows how I tend to think about measuring payoff, or success, of a particular solution with hypothetical scores (and yes, I've been accused of overthinking things many times before):

Notice that if you were to use this rubric, you'd be able to decide whether or not a particular category matters by moving the toggle on the far left, and you'd be able to set the values for "Actual" (How well does my visualization satisfy this factor currently?) and "Required" (How well does it need to satisfy this factor for me to achieve my goal?).

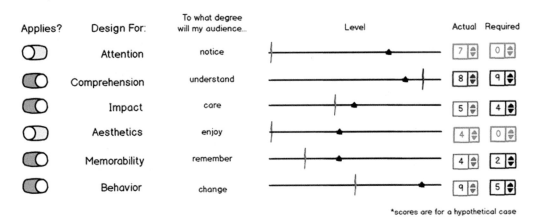

FIGURE 7.19   An example of how to determine which factors are important.

The "Actual" score would move the sliding triangle along the "Level" line from 0 to 10, and the "Required" value would determine where the target line is positioned similarly. Red target lines would correspond to factors that aren't met to a satisfactory level (triangles that lie to the *left* of the line), such as the target line for the "Comprehension" factor in the example.

It's pretty easy to conceive of situations, and I'd venture to say that most of us have experienced this first-hand, where a particular visualization type may have afforded increased precision of comparison, but that extra precision wasn't necessary for the task at hand, and the visualization was inferior in some other respect that doomed our efforts to failure.

Comprehensibility may be the single most important factor in data visualization, but I don't agree that it's the only factor we could potentially be concerned with. Not every data visualization scenario requires ultimate precision, just as engineers don't specify the same tight tolerances for a $15 scooter as they do for a $450M space shuttle.

Also, visualization types can make one type of comparison easier (say, part-to-whole) but another comparison more difficult (say, part-to-part).

Trade-Offs Abound

What seems clear, then, is that if we want to optimize using all of these variables (and likely others) for our particular scenario and audience, then we'll need to do a lot of work, and it will take a lot of time. If the audience is narrowly defined (say, for example, the board of directors of a specific nonprofit organization), then we simply can't test all of the variables (such as behavior – what will they do?) ahead of time. We have to forge ahead with imperfect information, and use something called bounded rationality – the idea that decision making involves inherent limitations in our knowledge, and we'll have to pick something that is "good enough."

And if we get the data at 11:30 a.m. and the meeting is at 3 p.m. on the same day? Running a battery of tests often just isn't practical.

But what if we feel that optimization is critical in a particular case? We can start by simplifying things for ourselves, focusing on just one or two input variables, making some key assumptions about who our audience will be, what their state of mind will be when we present to them, and how their reactions will be similar to or different from the reactions of a test audience. We reduce the degrees of freedom and optimize a much simpler equation. I'm all for knowing which chart types are more comprehensible than others. In a pinch, this is really good information to have at our disposal.

There Is Room for Both Approaches

Simon noted in his Nobel laureate speech that "decision makers can satisfice either by finding optimum solutions for a simplified world, or by finding satisfactory solutions for a more realistic world. Neither approach, in general, dominates the other, and both have continued to co-exist in the world of management science."[10]

I believe both should co-exist in the world of data visualization, too. We'll all be better off if people continue to test and find optimum visualizations for simplified and controlled scenarios in the lab, and we'll be better off if people continue to forge ahead and create "good enough" visualizations in the real world, taking into account a broader set of criteria and embracing the unknowns and messy uncertainties of communicating with other thinking and feeling human minds.

---

[10] https://www.jstor.org/stable/1808698?seq=1#page_scan_tab_contents.

Chapter Eight

Pitfall 7:
Design Dangers

"Design is not just what it looks like and feels like. Design is how it works."

—*Steve Jobs*

How We Dress up Data

I don't consider myself an expert designer – far from it – but I did have a unique opportunity in my career to encounter a high volume of very creative data visualizations over an extended period of time. I was asked to head up the global marketing team for the wildly popular and free Tableau Public platform,[1] and I held that role for over 5 years as it grew more than twenty-fold. It was a role I'm very grateful for, and one I'll never forget.

---

[1] https://public.tableau.com/.

What's so interesting about this platform is that it gives data nerds around the world a chance to apply the skills they develop in their day jobs to passion projects about topics that are interesting to them, from baseball team stats to multiple sclerosis dashboards, from sacred text word usage infographics to Santa Claus trackers. The topics range from silly to serious and the level of difficulty ranges from simple to sophisticated, and you can find everything in between those extremes.

And it isn't just corporate data jockeys set free to create without constraint. You'll also find the work of data journalists telling the stories of our time with data, corporate marketers creating engaging content for campaigns, government agencies giving citizens access to public data, and nonprofits bringing attention to their causes through interactive data.

All of these "authors" have two things in common: (1) they're publishing broadly to an audience on the web they don't entirely know and can't talk to en masse ahead of time, and (2) they can't assume that this audience will want to stop and look at anything they've created, or stick around for very long even if they do.

These two facts present an interesting design challenge that results in a need for both clarity and aesthetics. Since the work will potentially be seen by millions, it must be relatively easy to understand in order to accommodate the wide range of data literacy amongst the audience members. That's where clarity comes in. But since a lot of other online content is vying for the attention of those same millions of people, it must capture their attention and engage their imagination. Hence, the need for aesthetics, too.

I've long held the belief that both clarity and aesthetics matter when it comes to creating data graphics for an audience to consume.[2]

To attempt to define them in greater detail, the term "clarity" is fairly straightforward in this context. When I use that term in reference to data visualization, I'm referring to the speed and effectiveness

---

[2] https://dataremixed.com/2012/05/data-visualization-clarity-or-aesthetics/.

with which a data visualization imparts to the audience an accurate understanding of some fundamental truth about the real world. This has been scientifically researched a number of ways, including tests of cognition as well as eye-tracking studies and more.

While clarity may be easy to define, aesthetics, unfortunately, will never be so cooperative. Of course the problem with aesthetics is that the overused cliché "beauty is in the eye of the beholder" is very true. What looks beautiful to me here and now will not necessarily look beautiful to you, and may not even look beautiful to me at a different point in time.

Like fashion, certain elements of style come into vogue and then pass out of it again in a cycle that's hard to predict. And so we have a problem when it comes to defining aesthetics. The universal standards of "beautiful" elude us, and always have.

The previous chapter on graphical gaffes touched on both of these aspects, with a focus on clarity – choosing charts and creating them so that people can get a job done or come to an accurate understanding of the way things are. But it also touched on aesthetics – choosing color palettes that are simple and focus the reader's attention.

Design impacts both clarity and aesthetics. As Steve Jobs noted (see the epigraph to this chapter), we can't narrow the field of design to just aesthetics. How we interact with designed things and how they function also matter. Just as I learned in mechanical engineering school, we need to consider form, fit, and function in order to build something worth giving to the world.

So I'd like to break this chapter into two main parts. The first part will deal with pitfalls related to the look and feel of data visualizations. The second part will focus on pitfalls related to how we interact with them.

Pitfall 7A: Confusing Colors

A pitfall that's quite easy to fall into when creating dashboards with multiple charts and graphs is that of using color in ways that confuse people (Figure 8.1). There are many ways to confuse with color, including the oft-maligned red-green encoding that color-vision-deficient readers can't decipher. That's just one of many, though, and I'd like to illustrate three additional versions of the "confusing color" pitfall that I see people like me fall into quite often.

I'll conclude this section by talking about the design goal that I aspire to achieve any time I create a dashboard with multiple views.

2017 Boston Marathon Results

Top 10 Cities by Number of Finishers

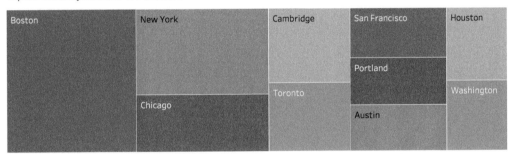

Number of Finishers by Official Time

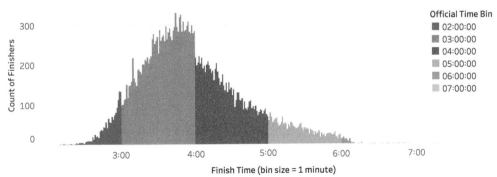

Source: https://www.kaggle.com/rojour/boston-results#marathon_results_2017.csv

FIGURE 8.1 A Boston Marathon dashboard that uses the same color for different attributes.

Color Pitfall 1: Using the Same Color for Two Different Variables

The example for the first type of this common pitfall comes from a marathon dashboard showing the results of the 2017 Boston Marathon. The data for this race is available online.[3]

Here are some pluses (things I like) and deltas (things I would change) about this dashboard:

Pluses: I like the use of color in the histogram that shows the clear cutoff points, where finishers cross the line in droves immediately before the turning of the hour, especially the fourth hour of the race. This shows how goal-setting can affect the performance of a population, and it's fascinating.

Deltas: Notice that the same red hue, though, applies to finishers from Chicago and Portland, and also to people who finished the race between 4 and 5 hours. Likewise, the same orange is used to encode the finishers from New York and Austin, as well as people who finished between 3 and 4 hours after starting. Similarly, teal, blue, and green have multiple meanings. Of course, there's no actual relation between these particular groups, though it may seem like there is at first glance.

To avoid this confusion, I propose using entirely different color schemes for the histogram and the treemap (and not repeating any colors within the treemap itself), or, better yet, not putting these two charts next to each other at all, because they tell completely different stories.

Color Pitfall 2: Using the Same Color Saturation for Different Magnitudes of the Same Variable

Similarly, I've made the mistake of using the same color saturation to effectively create two conflicting color legends for the exact same dashboard. Consider this trivial map that I created with data about mileage of California roads by county to illustrate the point (Figure 8.2).

---

[3] https://www.kaggle.com/rojour/boston-results#marathon_results_2017.csv.

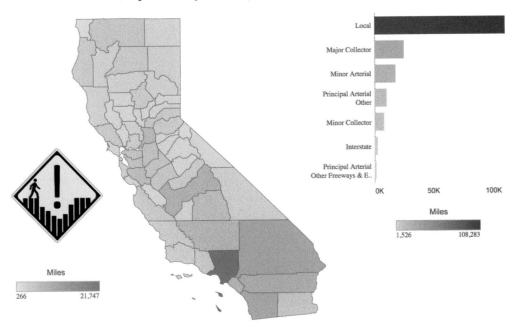

FIGURE 8.2 A dashboard with two different sequential color palettes using the same hue.

Notice that there are two different sequential color legends on the dashboard that use the exact same turquoise color. In the filled map, the fully saturated turquoise color corresponds to a specific county (Los Angeles County) with 21,747 total miles of roads.

In the bar chart, the full turquoise color saturation corresponds to a specific road type (Local roads) with a total of 108,283 miles for the entire state of California. Just eyeing the dashboard in passing, however, the viewer may connect Los Angeles County with local roads and mistakenly think these two marks are connected. Or, the reader may look at the wrong color legend (if both are in fact included) and be misled about how many miles of road the county actually includes, or vice versa.

From a software user's perspective, this pitfall was incredibly easy to fall into because all I had to do was click and drag the "Miles" data field over to the field that determines color of the map, and also do the same in the place where I created and edited the bar chart. These two visualizations are aggregating miles by totally different dimensions – county and road type – but I can easily create a confusing color encoding if I'm not paying close attention.

Is there a way to avoid this type of color pitfall?

Notice that the color encoding on the bar chart is actually redundant. We already know the relative proportions of the miles of different road types by the lengths of their corresponding bars, which is quite effective all by itself. Why also include miles on the color shelf, especially considering the fact that the color would conflict with the choropleth map, where color is totally necessary?

To eliminate this conflicting color scheme, let's remove color from the bars altogether and just leave an outline around them (Figure 8.3).

Color Pitfall 3: Using Too Many Color Encodings on One Dashboard

It's very common to use too many color schemes on a dashboard, especially with big corporate dashboards where the various stakeholders call for everything but the kitchen sink to be added to the view.

Figure 8.4 shows a dashboard I created to illustrate the point – my first dashboard that uses the Sales SuperStore sample dashboard that comes with Tableau Desktop.

In this dashboard we see not just one red-green color encoding but *two*, and they have different extremes for the exact same measure (Profit). We also see red and green used in the scatterplot, but now they refer to two of the four different regions (West and South, respectively) instead of different profit levels. Finally, we have another bar chart that uses no color scheme, but each bar is blue – the same blue as the Central region in the scatterplot.

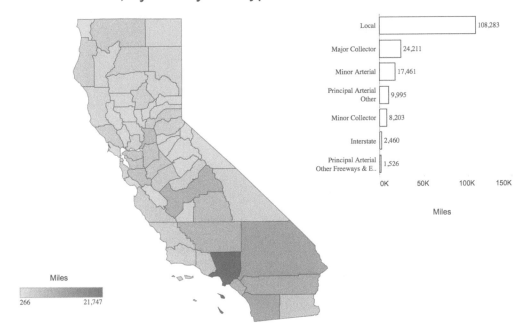

FIGURE 8.3 A version of the dashboard using only one sequential color encoding to avoid confusion.

You get the point. This isn't what we want to create. I think I broke all of the rules in creating this one.

My Design Aspiration: Only One Color Encoding per Dashboard

This goal isn't always feasible, but as much as possible, I try to include one and only one color scheme on every dashboard I create. The reason is that I find it takes me a lot longer to figure out what's going on in someone else's dashboard when they've used more than one. It's that simple.

This means I often have to make a tough choice: which is the variable (quantitative or categorical) that will be blessed with the one and only one color encoding on the dashboard? It'll become the

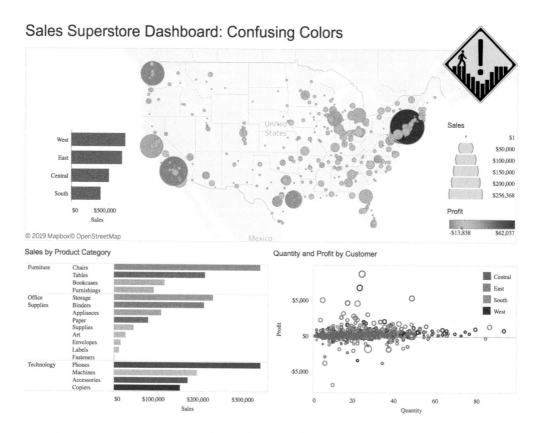

FIGURE 8.4   A company sales dashboard using a fabricated store data set.

variable that receives the most attention, so it should be the one that's most related to the primary task the user will perform when using the dashboard.

For example, if the dashboard was created for a sales meeting in which the directors of each U.S. sales region talk about what's working well and what's not working well in their respective regions, then the "Region" attribute could very well take the honored place of prominence (Figure 8.5).

Notice that this version of the dashboard doesn't show which cities were unprofitable overall. We have shown profit by product category as a separate bar chart in the bottom left, but the map no longer gives us any information about profit. So this version

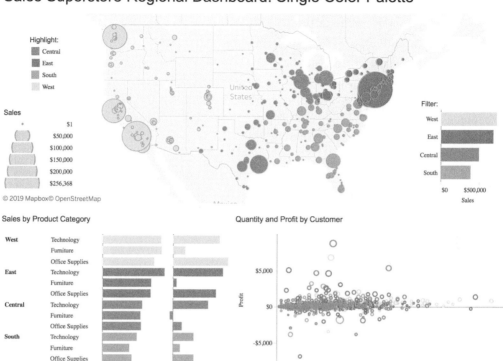

FIGURE 8.5 A redesigned version of the dashboard that limits use to a single-color encoding.

of the dashboard actually shows less information, but shows it in a way that's easier to understand. Sales executives are typically more focused on sales, aka the "top line," than profit, or the "bottom line."

But if we were to find out the profit by city was critical to the discussion, we'd need to either find a way to add it back to the dashboard, or we'd need to create a second view to handle this part of the discussion.

Trying to cram all of the information that could possibly be needed into a single view is often unnecessary, and what results in the type of color confusion we're talking about in this section.

Pitfall 7B: Omitted Opportunities

You'll recall that back in Chapter 4 (the chapter all about our third pitfall, mathematical miscues) we showed how a very common software default led us to completely miss the fact that one particularly moody and haunting poet didn't publish anything in three different years during the course of his career. We missed this fact because the years were missing from the view since there were no records in the data set with those years.

We showed how to correct this chart setting in order to avoid this pitfall, as shown in Figure 4.8, which I will share again in Figure 8.6.

But what I didn't mention in that chapter is that this version of the chart has omitted much more than just a few years on the x-axis. It omits a palpable aesthetic design opportunity.

For those of you familiar with the poetry and stories of Edgar Allan Poe, many are moody and melancholy and some are even downright chilling or haunting. But there's nothing particularly moody or

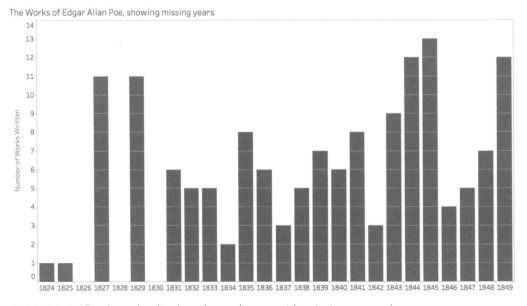

FIGURE 8.6   Poe's works displayed as columns with missing years shown.

melancholy about this chart at all, and certainly nothing chilling or even remotely haunting. It's a nice, bright blue column chart with divisions for each published work, creating a stacked box feel. It does nothing to evoke the feeling of Edgar Allan Poe's work, and there are no artistic elements that draw in the reader or communicate the subject matter to them in any way.

This is another sin of omission. A major one.

Whenever I ask people in my classes how they would change this view to add some artistic flair, they often suggest changing the squares into books so that there would be a stacked book feel. I like that idea, but his published works are of widely varying length, and some of them are incredibly short, so that might be a bit misleading.

What we can do, though, is turn the y-axis upside down so that the squares stack *downward*, and we can change the color from bright blue to red, evoking a dripping, blood-stained feel (Figure 8.7).

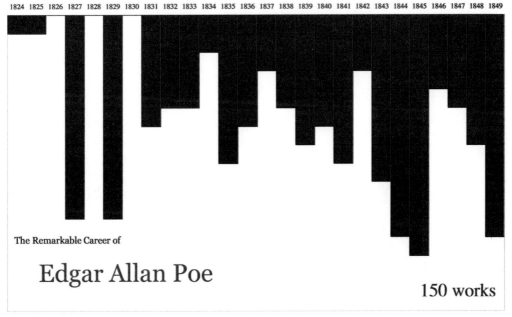

FIGURE 8.7 A modified version of the Poe chart that adds aesthetic elements.

We need to be very careful with reversing axes. If the marks were lines instead of bars, the slope would appear to go *down* at the precise time that the measure *increases*. So, I very rarely find occasions to invert axes for line charts.

Once instance where such a change may be warranted is when showing change in rank over time. Since low numbers like 1 and 2 correspond to high ranks, and high numbers like 99 or 100 correspond to low ranks, inverting the y-axis actually helps show when a particular item or group goes up or down in rank (Figure 8.8).

Wouldn't it be strange if the tenth-ranked skill were at the top of the chart and the top-ranked skill were at the bottom? I would make

LinkedIn: The Skills Companies Need the Most

See how the Top Skills ranking as published by LinkedIn has changed over the course of the past five years. Hover over each circle to see the skill ranked, and click to read the analysis.

FIGURE 8.8   A "bumps chart" showing ranking of skills over time.

the argument that this type of chart is one where inverting the axis actually aides cognition and comparisons.

The Poe chart is an example where inverting the axis doesn't either help or hinder comprehension dramatically, but it certainly does help with the aesthetic look and feel of the chart. We still get the sense that there are more works published in years where the boxes stack farther downward, just as there would be more blood on the mirror if the drip went all the way to the bottom.

A key point, though, is that I'd hesitate to add artistic flair whenever doing so results in a dramatic *reduction* in clarity or comprehensibility, or when adding aesthetic elements is likely to totally mislead some of my audience. These are trade-offs to be aware of and to test with potential audience members, even if the test is just a quick-and-dirty one.

In this case, though, we can go farther than simply inverting the y-axis. There is a nice gap in the very center of the chart. It's a gift from the data gods that we can use to great aesthetic advantage. While I don't think we should fill every single white space (quite the contrary in fact) this one is just begging for an image of the author himself. Luckily for us, a nice oval portrait image of Edgar Allan Poe is available in public domain and free to use under the Creative Commons license. So is an image of his signature, which is a nice object to replace the text of his name, and very appropriate because these works would have been written by hand, not word processor (Figure 8.9).

These images aren't just useless chartjunk. They actually convey information. His image will be recognizable to many (although not all) of our audience. For those who have seen his photo before and are familiar with his face, seeing again here will convey the subject matter and also bring back to the surface memories and feelings associated with reading his poems in our high school textbooks. There is real value in that experience we have created.

It's so easy to miss opportunities like this, and fall into yet another pitfall of omission. The key to avoiding this pitfall is to allow our

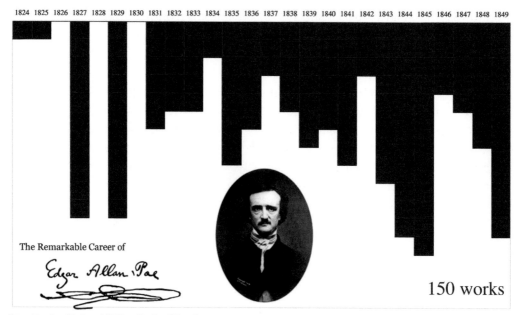

1824 1825 1826 1827 1828 1829 1830 1831 1832 1833 1834 1835 1836 1837 1838 1839 1840 1841 1842 1843 1844 1845 1846 1847 1848 1849

The Remarkable Career of

Edgar Allan Poe

150 works

Source: https://en.wikipedia.org/wiki/Edgar_Allan_Poe_bibliography
Image: https://en.wikipedia.org/wiki/Edgar_Allan_Poe#/media/File:Edgar_Allan_Poe_2_retouched_and_transparent_bg.png   Ben Jones, 7 October 2015

FIGURE 8.9   A modified version of the dashboard that adds images to further enhance aesthetic appeal.

creative juices to flow, and to ask ourselves what opportunities exist to add aesthetic components that will enhance the overall experience for our audience.

Great care must be taken when seeking to avoid this pitfall for two reasons. The first reason was already mentioned: there can be a trade-off between clarity and aesthetics at play, which we will want to approach with caution. The second is that sometimes our audience doesn't want any of these elements whatsoever. There are people for whom these types of visual enhancements are actually annoying, and they will get very irritated with you if you add them.

I'll never forget the time I gave an hour-long presentation to a group of people who worked at a city office in Arizona about how they could apply creative techniques similar to this one to their reports and dashboards. At the end of the presentation, I asked whether there was anyone in the audience who felt that there were zero opportunities in their current role to make use of such creative elements.

One woman raised her hand. She said she worked for the police department and prepared their weekly reports. She felt that any attempt to add creative or aesthetically pleasing elements would backfire spectacularly. I had no interest in getting her fired from her job, but I asked her to think about it as time went along, to challenge that assumption. I'd like to say she added some fancy thing or two to a dashboard and got applauded by all the grouchy chartjunk-hating chiefs of the force, but I haven't talked to her since that presentation. Sorry if that's a disappointing end to the story. For the record, I still think she can do it.

Pitfall 7C: Usability Uh-Ohs

Of course, design is about much more than simply color choice, aesthetic elements, and how something looks. Just like this chapter's epigraph states, it's also about how it works. Think form, fit, and function.

I've been educated and inspired by the best-selling design classic *The Design of Everyday Things* by user-centered design guru Don Norman.[4] You really have to read the entire book, which applies to all types of objects that people design, from chairs to doors to software to organizational structures. It provides thoughtful and practical principles that guide designers to design all of those things well. By "well" he means "products that fit the needs and capabilities of people" (p. 218).

As I read it, it occurred to me that data visualizations are "everyday things" now, too, even richly interactive ones viewed on tablets and phones. That has only become the case in the past decade or so. Yes, examples can be traced back to the early days of the Internet,

---

[4] https://www.amazon.com/Design-Everyday-Things-Revised-Expanded/dp/0465050654/.

but the recent explosion of data, software tools, and programming libraries has caused their proliferation.

And I found that point after point, principle after principle in Norman's book applied directly to data visualization. I'd like to call out five points that struck me as particularly relevant to the field of data visualization.

1. Good Visualizations Are Discoverable and Understandable

Norman starts his book describing two important characteristics of all designed products:

- **Discoverability:** Is it possible even to figure out what actions are achievable and where and how to perform them?
- **Understanding:** What does it all mean? How is the product supposed to be used? What do all the different controls and settings mean?

He talks about common things that are often anything but discoverable and understandable, such as faucets, doors, and stovetops. One of my favorite quotes in the book is about faucets (p. 150):

If you want the faucet to be pushed, make it look as if it should be pushed.

It occurred to me that the typical stovetop design snafu has a direct translation into the world of data visualization. To explain, let's start with the problem with stovetops. Ever turn on the wrong burner? Why? Because you're stupid? No. Because there are often poor mappings between the controls and the burners. The burners are sometimes arranged in a two-by-two grid while the controls can be in a straight line (Figure 8.10).

What does that have to do with data visualization? We often use similar controls – radio buttons, combo boxes, sliders, and so on – to filter and highlight the marks in the view. When there are multiple views in a visualization (a dashboard), there's a similar opportunity to provide clear, or natural, mappings.

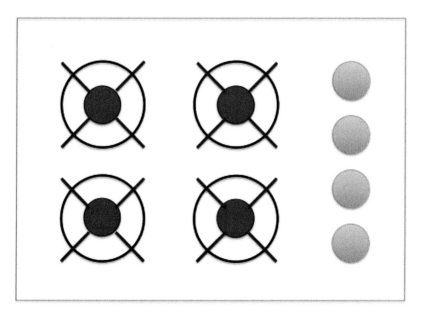

A common stovetop design, with no natural mapping between
burners (grid) and controls (linear)

FIGURE 8.10 A common stovetop design, with no natural mapping
between burners and controls.

Norman gives the following advice for mappings:

- **Best mapping:** Controls are mounted directly on the item to be controlled.
- **Second-best mapping:** Controls are as close as possible to the object to be controlled.
- **Third-best mapping:** Controls are arranged in the same spatial configuration as the objects to be controlled.

Often the software default places the controls on the right-hand side. Here's my attempt (Figure 8.11) to show these options on a generic data dashboard, where the four different views are labeled A, B, C, and D, and the controls that change them are labeled according to the views they modify.

This is a relatively straightforward example, and the job of the designer of a more complex visualization is to make it similarly clear

A Common Default

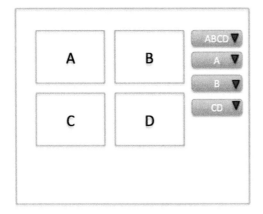

All filters placed on the right regardless of what view they control, indicated by matching letter(s)

A Natural Mapping

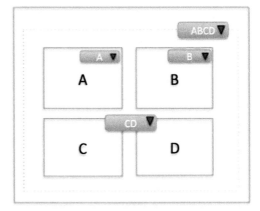

Filters placed in close proximity to the views they control, indicated by matching letter(s).

FIGURE 8.11   An example of default versus natural mapping of filters on a data dashboard.

what can be done and how to do it. Designers use things like affordances, signifiers, constraints, and mappings to make it obvious. Note that it takes a lot of effort to make the complex obvious.

2. Don't Blame People for Getting Confused or Making Errors

A fundamental principle that Norman drives home a number of times in the book is that human error usually isn't the fault of humans, but rather of poorly designed systems. Here are two great quotes on the topic (p. 167):

> It is not possible to eliminate human error if it is thought of as a personal failure rather than as a sign of poor design of procedures or equipment.

And again on the same page:

> If the system lets you make the error, it is badly designed. And if the system induces you to make the error, it is really badly designed. When I turn on the wrong stove burner, it is not due to my lack of knowledge: It is due to poor mapping between controls and burners.

Norman differentiates between two types of errors: slips and mistakes.

- **Slips** are when you mean to do one thing, but you do another.
- **Mistakes** are when you come up with the wrong goal or plan and then carry it out.

Both types of errors happen when people interact with data visualizations. In the world of mobile, slips are so common – maybe I meant to tap that small icon at the edge of my phone screen, but the phone and app recognized a tap of an adjacent icon instead.

Mistakes are also common. Maybe it made sense to me to filter to a subset of the data to get my answer, but in reality I was misleading myself by introducing a selection bias that wasn't appropriate at all. If someone makes the wrong decision based on misinformation they took from your visualization, that's your problem at least as much as it is theirs, if not more so.

How to make sure your readers avoid slips and mistakes? Build and test. Iterate. Watch people interact with your visualization. When they screw up, don't blame them or step in and explain what they did wrong and why they should've known better. Write it down and go back to the drawing board. If the person who agreed to test your visualization made that error, don't you think many more likely will? And you won't be there to tell them all what they did wrong. Your only chance to fix the error is to prevent it.

3. Designing for Pleasure and Emotion Is Important

I'm a big believer in this principle. Norman states that "great designers make pleasurable experiences" (p. 10):

> Experience is critical for it determines how fondly people remember their interactions. Was the overall experience positive, or was it frustrating and confusing?

How can an experience with a data visualization be pleasurable? In lots of ways. It can make it easy to understand something interesting or important about our world, it can employ good design techniques and artistic elements, it can surprise us with a clever or funny metaphor, or some combination of these and more.

Remember our ridiculous discussion of a hypothetical pie chart with 333 slices in the previous chapter? Well, here's a dashboard about bicycle parking stands in Dublin, Ireland, that contains a pie chart with exactly that many slices, one for each stand, sized by the occupancy, or the number of bikes that can be parked in each one (Figure 8.12).

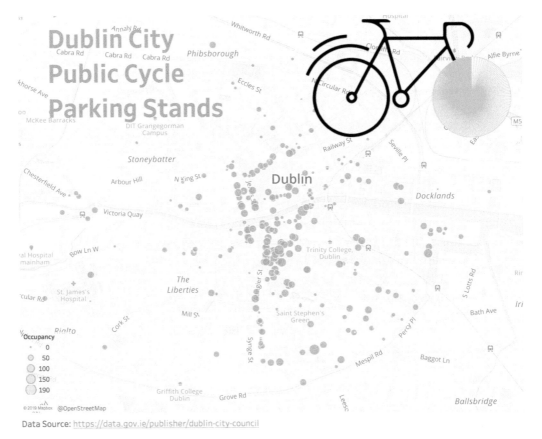

Data Source: https://data.gov.ie/publisher/dublin-city-council

FIGURE 8.12 A dashboard of bicycle stands in Dublin that uses an outrageous pie chart in a fun way.

You can use it to hover over a slice or a dot on the map to see the occupancy of each stand, and where it ranks in the overall list of 333 stands. Is that such a travesty? I think it's kind of neat.

What about emotion, the "*e-word*" to which the analytical folks in our midst can sometimes be allergic? Cognition gets a lot of play in the world of data visualization while emotion does not. But these two horses of the chariot that is the human spirit are actually inextricably yoked (p. 47):

> *Cognition and emotion cannot be separated. Cognitive thoughts lead to emotions: emotions drive cognitive thoughts.*
>
> *Cognition attempts to make sense of the world: emotion assigns value.... Cognition provides understanding: emotion provides value judgments.*

So let's embrace emotions. Some data visualizations make us angry or upset. Some make us laugh out loud. Some are just delightful to interact with. These elements of the experience should be part of the discourse in our field, and not ignored. If we take them into consideration, we'll probably design better stuff.

4. Complexity Is Good, Confusion Is Bad

There's a trend in data visualization to move away from the big, complex dashboards of 2010 and toward "lightweight" and uber-simple individual graphs, and even GIFs. Why? A big part of the reason is that they work better on mobile. Also, we've learned in the past few years that the complexity of those big dashboards isn't always necessary.

This is a great development and I'm all for it, but let's just remember that there was often a great value to the rich interaction that's still possible on a larger screen. Instead of abandoning rich interactivity altogether, I believe we should be looking for new and innovative ways to give these advanced capabilities to readers on smaller devices. When those capabilities will help us achieve some goal, we'll be better off. We're not there yet.

After all, it's not the complexity of the detailed, filterable dashboard that's the problem on the smartphone screen – it's that we haven't figured out how to make these capabilities intuitive to a reader on this device yet, and the experience is confusing.

I actually see this as a good thing. Our generation has the chance to figure this out for the generations to come. The growth of the numerical literacy of our population will be well worth the effort.

5. Absolute Precision Isn't Always Necessary

I have to be honest. This one is my hot button. There's a school of thought that says that the visualization type that gives the reader the ability to guess the true proportions of the thing visualized with the greatest accuracy is the only one that can be used. Some go so far as to declare it immoral to choose a visualization type that introduces any more error than another (they all have some error).

I found this great visualization about different encoding channels in Tamara Munzner's book *Visualization Analysis and Design* (Figure 8.13).

This research shows that all encoding types are imperfect. People won't guess the true proportions with 100% accuracy for any of them. And many times absolute precision just isn't necessary – not for a task they need to perform, and not for a general awareness we're trying to impart.

If we had to pick the one with the highest accuracy all the time, we'd only ever have dot plots, bar charts, and line charts and that's it.

The problem with this line of reasoning is that absolute precision isn't always necessary for the task at hand. Norman uses the example of converting temperature from Celsius to Fahrenheit. If all you need to do is figure out whether you'll need to wear a sweater when you go outside, a shortcut approximate conversion equation is good enough. It doesn't matter whether it's 52°F, 55°F, 55.8°F, or 55.806°F. In all four cases, you're wearing a light sweater.

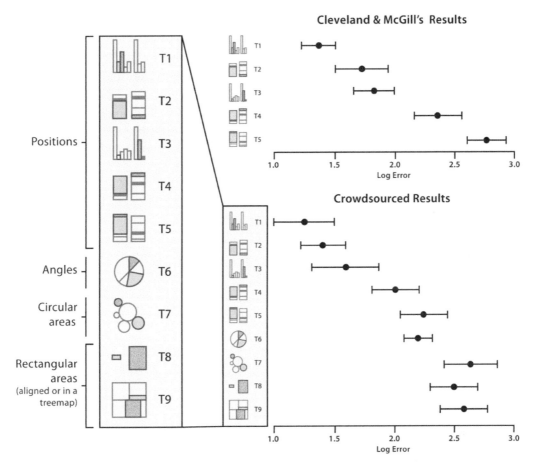

FIGURE 8.13 Research results showing error involved with different encoding types.

Since there are errors associated with every visualization type, and since we aren't machines or perfect decoders of pixels or ink, then sometimes it's okay that a general understanding is achieved. Many times this means we are free to add interesting chart types that lend flavor and, heaven forbid, even a little bit of fun to the endeavor.

I think that's a good thing. In the Tableau Public role, I certainly saw many people use creativity to great effect. When I started in that role in 2013, I think there were still many people in the business intelligence space who felt that any aesthetic component or artistic flair was inherently evil and to be avoided. By the time I left, this attitude had changed, and it seemed to me, at least, that people creating dashboards both for public consumption as well as for corporate reporting were feeling empowered to find those aesthetic elements that would take a piece of work to the next level.

We'll see how much longer that trend continues, and whether it will turn out to be a pendulum that swings a little too far.

Chapter Nine

Conclusion

"Mistakes are a fact of life. It is the response to error that counts."

—*Nikki Giovanni*

Well, we've traveled a long road together, and we've considered many aspects of the data working pathway, both pinnacles of wonder and pitfalls of despair. And if you're like me, you have a looming sense that the types of mistakes we've mapped out in this book are only the beginning.

The fact is, they're necessary in order for us to grow.

To drive this point home, I'd like to relate a famous story to you that I've only ever seen attributed to an anonymous source.

There once was a journalist who was interviewing a wealthy and successful bank president.

"Sir," he said, "what is the secret to your success?"
"Two words," replied the bank president.
"And what are they, sir?" asked the journalist.
"Good decisions," replied the president.
"And how, sir, do you make good decisions?"
'One word."
"And what word is that?"
"Experience."
"And how do you get experience?"
"Two words."
"And what are they, sir?"
"Bad decisions."

Working with data involves lots of decisions. Some of them are good decisions and some of them are bad decisions. It's not reasonable to expect ourselves and others to only ever make good decisions. We're going to make mistakes on the road to success with data, just as sure as we're going to come across data that's flawed and dirty. It's the way things are.

We can choose how we react to this state of affairs. We can throw in the towel right now. Why try? Or we can stick our head in the sand and pretend we don't make the kinds of mistakes that all the other knuckleheads out there seem to make so often. *Sheesh*. Or we can beat ourselves up every time we fall into a data pitfall. "How could I be so stupid?"

Or we can pick ourselves up, recognize the mistake, accept that it happened, put a little tick on the tick sheet, investigate – without judging – how and why we didn't catch it upfront this time, and tell ourselves it's going to be okay. I believe that you and I are far less likely to make this mistake the next time around if we react like this.

I'll never forget a time when I was a young mechanical design engineer at an automotive sensor company in Southern California. My boss, Mr. Chen, was a very wise man, sort of like an amused father or grandfather who mentored me with care. This company had been struggling financially for some time. No one had been getting raises. Layoffs seemed imminent. They had even begun counting rolls of toilet paper. It was a tough spell for the company.

There was a time in just my third month on the job when I was responsible for creating a batch of sensors in the lab that were going to be sold to a customer. It was a small batch, but the value of the raw materials added up to about $15,000, which at that time was about a third of my entry-level engineer salary. The sensors needed to be calibrated before they were cured in the oven and the assembly completed. The drawings were clear about that.

But I messed it up. I told the technicians, who made far less money than I did, to go ahead and finish off the assemblies, thinking that we could calibrate the sensors afterward. We couldn't, and the batch was ruined. Hundreds of high-precision sensors had to be thrown in the big scrap bin in the back of the building. *Ouch*.

I realized right away with a sinking feeling of dread that the error was mine, not the technicians'. I made up my mind that I would tell my boss, preparing myself for the obvious outcome that I would be fired on the spot. I had a pregnant wife at the time, and the temptation to cover it up or blame someone else was enormous.

When I told Mr. Chen what had happened, he walked up to the lab with me, drawings in hand. He and I went around and he asked the technicians what had happened. They looked at me, looked at the drawings, and then at Mr. Chen, and told them that I had provided different instructions than what the drawings said. I nodded in agreement, and said they weren't to blame.

Mr. Chen and I went back to his office, and we each took a seat. Before he had a chance to say anything, I asked him if he was going to fire me for the costly mistake. He smiled and said, "Are you kidding me? I just paid $15,000 for you to be trained on how not to calibrate a batch of sensors. I can't afford to pay another junior engineer to learn that same lesson."

Obviously, I was relieved. And it's true, I had learned a valuable lesson about how to calibrate pressure sensors for heavy-duty trucks. But I learned something even more valuable – that making mistakes is inevitable, that there's no sense in browbeating yourself or another person for making one, and that if you think of it as a training cost, it turns the whole mess around.

So it's my sincere hope that you aren't discouraged by all the possible ways to get it wrong. That's not my purpose in writing this book at all. Quite the contrary. Possibility of failure is built into the very nature of our world, but we can't let this fact, while daunting, totally confine us to the sofa.

Data is going to be a huge part of the future of our species on this planet. In our generation it has increased in importance by leaps and bounds in a very short amount of time, and this trend is showing no sign of abating. We're in the infant phase of the data-working lifespan of our species.

Let's think about babies for a minute. A newborn's immune system learns to fight harmful viruses for the first time. A newborn grows into a toddler who learns to avoid walking into the coffee table or falling down the stairs. A toddler becomes a young child who learns not to touch the stovetop. These early experiences lead a human being to develop a strong immune system, a keen sense of balance, and an aversion to sharp objects or hot surfaces.

That's what we're doing for future generations right now, as it relates to data. It's up to us to continue to face these potential pitfalls, to learn from them, to build a better sense of where they are, what they look like, and how to avoid them. We're building the immune system, the defense mechanisms, and the habits of our species to make good use of data without shooting ourselves in the foot. If future generations look back at our mistakes and roll their eyes or shake their heads in derision, then we'll have done our part.

This book is just the beginning. It's a brief catalog of the ones I've come across in my data working days so far. I imagine it amounts to a small portion of the total number of different kinds of pitfalls I will come across before my lifetime is over. I have many more things to learn, and I'll keep jotting down new pitfalls that I come across – hopefully some of them from the top looking down.

And I'd love to know if you think I've missed any big ones, or if I've gotten any of these wrong. I bet I have. As ego-bruising as that would be to fall into a pitfall while writing a book about pitfalls, I'm prepared for that. So don't hold back.

As promised, I've created a checklist for you to use as a set of reminders about these pitfalls, and how to avoid them. By all means change it or add to it to suit your purposes. It's a living document, and it's as susceptible to falling into the very pitfalls it's seeking to help you avoid.

All the best to you on your journey to a higher place!

Avoiding Data Pitfalls Checklist

Pitfall 1: Epistemic Errors: *How we think about data*
- [ ] 1A. The Data Reality Gap: Identify ways in which the data is different than reality.
- [ ] 1B. All Too Human Data: Identify any human-keyed data and associated processes.
- [ ] 1C. Inconsistent Ratings: Test the repeatability and reproducibility of ratings and measurements.
- [ ] 1D. The Black Swan Pitfall: See if you're making any inductive leaps to universal statements.
- [ ] 1E. The God Pitfall: Ask whether hypotheses formed and statements made are falsifiable.

Pitfall 2: Technical Trespasses: *How we process data*
- [ ] 2A. Dirty Data: Consider the values in each variable, visualize the data, and scan for anomalies.
- [ ] 2B. Bad Blends and Joins: Investigate the input and output of every join, blend, and union.

Pitfall 3: Mathematical Miscues: *How we calculate data*

☐ 3A. Aggravating Aggregations: Explore the contours of your data and look for partial categories.

☐ 3B. Missing Values: Scan for nulls and look for missing values between adjacent category levels.

☐ 3C. Tripping on Totals: Determine whether any category levels or rows are totals or subtotals.

☐ 3D. Preposterous Percents: Consider numerators and denominators of all added rates and percents.

☐ 3E. Unmatching Units: Check that formulas involve variables with the correct units of measure.

Pitfall 4: Statistical Slipups: *How we compare data*

☐ 4A. Descriptive Debacles: Consider distributions when communicating mean, median, or mode.

☐ 4B. Inferential Infernos: When inferring about populations, verify statistical significance.

☐ 4C. Slippery Sampling: Make sure samples are random, unbiased, and, if necessary, stratified.

☐ 4D. Insensitivity to Sample Size: Look for very small sample sizes, occurrences, or rates.

Pitfall 5: Analytical Aberrations: *How we analyze data*

☐ 5A. The Intuition/Analysis False Dichotomy: Ask whether you're honoring your human intuition.

☐ 5B. Exuberant Extrapolations: Check for times that you're projecting far into the future.

☐ 5C. Ill-Advised Interpolations: Consider if there should be more values between adjacent ones.

☐ 5D. Funky Forecasts: Think about how you're forecasting values, and whether that's valid.

☐ 5E. Moronic Measures: Check whether what you're measuring and visualizing really matters.

Pitfall 6: Graphical Gaffes: *How we visualize data*

- ☐ 6A. Challenging Charts: Identify the core purpose of your visual and validate that it achieves it.
- ☐ 6B. Data Dogmatism: Ask whether you've failed to consider a valid solution due to rigid rules.
- ☐ 6C. The Optimize/Satisfice False Dichotomy: Decide if you need to optimize or satisfice.

Pitfall 7: Design Dangers: *How we dress up data*

- ☐ 7A. Confusing Colors: Strive for one and only one color encoding; add another only if you must.
- ☐ 7B. Omitted Opportunities: Stop and consider adding judicious embellishment of charts.
- ☐ 7C. Usability Uh-Ohs: Test whether those using your visualization can actually use it well.

Pitfall 8: Biased Baseline: *Who has a voice in data*

- ☐ 8A. The Unheard Voice: Make sure you are hearing and considering voices that have historically been undervalued or ignored.

The Pitfall of the Unheard Voice

Hello, dear reader. I am sitting here on my couch near Seattle, on a sunny Sunday morning in July after having read through the edits and proofs of each of the nine chapters of a draft version of this book. I have made a ghastly realization that is giving me pause to reflect and ask myself some important questions.

I knew when I set out to write this book that I would be sure to fall into numerous pitfalls while writing a book about pitfalls. I steeled myself against this ironic inevitability, and decided I would need to be the doctor who takes his own medicine: learn to laugh about it and move on as a wiser person.

But I'm not laughing about this one. I've discovered that I've fallen into an egregious pitfall that I didn't include or describe anywhere in the pages of this book. It wouldn't be accurate to say that this pitfall went unnoticed for ages, because the vast majority didn't even see it as a pitfall at all until recently. They saw it as the right and best path to take.

What is this pitfall I'm talking about? Did you notice that the checklist above included an eighth type of pitfall? Look again if you didn't.

There are nine chapters in this book, and these nine chapters each have a quote at the beginning – an epigraph. Researching and choosing an epigraph is a part of the writing process that I really enjoy, because I get to scan the thoughts and words of brilliant people and take inspiration from them. It's a very rewarding process for me.

But the first draft of this book contained nine quotes from nine men. There was not a single inspirational quote from a woman.

None.

Zero.

How did this happen? How did I not come to select even one quote from a woman in the initial writing of this book, *which took place over the course of four years*?

Even worse, how did I not even realize it until the very end, with the printers warming up and getting ready to send my book to people around the world, including women of all ages who are looking to build data skills and contribute to this booming data dialogue around us?

How would I feel if I were one of them and I got my hands on a copy of the book and wondered what it would take for my voice to be heard?

I feel strongly enough about this pitfall that I decided not only to fix it, but to write about it in the hopes that I can help raise awareness about it among my fellow males in the data world.

This pitfall is endemic in our discipline, in the broader STEM world, and in Western society at large. At the time I'm writing this, only 17% of the 1.5 million Wikipedia biography pages are about women.[1]

The voices of talented women have been ignored for too long, and too often their contributions have been attributed to men. I'm currently working on an article for the *Nightingale,* the new journal published by the Data Visualization Society, about a twentieth-century data visualization practitioner and author named Mary Eleanor Spear. In 1969, she wrote a fabulous book I've recently discovered called *Practical Charting Techniques*, and I'm currently awaiting shipment of an earlier book of hers titled *Charting Statistics*, published in 1952.

Why do I mention Spear in this final section on unheard voices? For starters, there is, of course, no Wikipedia page for her at the time I'm writing this sentence (a fact that will soon change).

But it's more than that. There's a common and popular statistical chart type called the box plot that depicts the quartiles of quantitative data in a compact and convenient way. If you research its origin, you'll find that the innovation of the box plot is commonly attributed to mathematician John W. Tukey, who "introduced this type of visual data display in 1969."[2]

At present, the name Mary Eleanor Spear is not to be found anywhere on the Wikipedia page about the box plot, even though her name can be found in research papers on the topic of this chart type.[3]

---

[1] https://www.thelily.com/wikipedia-has-15-million-biographies-in-english-only-17-percent-are-about-women/.
[2] https://en.wikipedia.org/wiki/Box_plot.
[3] https://vita.had.co.nz/papers/boxplots.pdf.

But her name should be there. In her 1952 book, Spear depicted an early version of the box plot, which she called the range-bar. This was evidently a chart type that Tukey modified to create the box plot we know and use today.

While many see Tukey's modifications as helpful, why is Spear's name so often left out of the discussion of the origin of this chart? If Tukey had improved upon the work of another man, would that man's name have been left out of the record? Why did I first hear of her name just a few months ago, in spite of working in the business intelligence industry for over a decade?

And why, as I'm looking to go back and include quotes by women for the epigraphs of each chapter of this book, do I find so few of them? Why, in an article that purports to list the "100 greatest data quotes," are the words of only seven women to be found?[4] That's just one article. There were many other "top 20" or "top whatever" data and analytics quote lists I found that included no women whatsoever.

These are questions we have to ask ourselves. It just shouldn't be that way, and I'm mortified to think that I almost perpetuated this incredible bias in this book with lazily selected epigraphs. There was nothing wrong with the quotes I originally selected. They were brilliant thoughts from brilliant people. And I'm not seeking to take away anything from them, or from Tukey, or from those who have taken time to compile helpful quotes for all of us.

But it's time to start amplifying voices that have traditionally been drowned out. Voices of all types. A tradition that filters out so many bright contributors is much too costly. Imagine a world where people's thoughts are heard and considered in proportion to the value of the words themselves, as opposed to the value the culture places on the demographic of the person who said them. Wouldn't this be a better world?

What can we do to move our world in that direction? Let's do that.

---

[4] https://analyticsweek.com/content/100-greatest-data-quotes/.

Index

Page references followed by f indicate an illustrated figure.